RESPONSIBLE GROWTH FOR THE NEW MILLENNIUM

Integrating Society, Ecology, and the Economy

THE WORLD BANK
Washington, D.C.

CONTENTS

Figures

Tables

FOREWORD

This volume offers a vision of the mid-twenty-first century that highlights the challenges that the international community will face in achieving balanced, equitable, and sustainable development. It forces us to consider a key question: how do we sustain achievements toward the Millennium Development Goals adopted by the international community beyond the target date of 2015?

Today, the majority of citizens in developing countries see a world troubled by poverty, social inequity, distrust, terror, and lack of confidence in governance systems. The link between poverty and inequality, plus the high correlation between race, gender, youth, and poverty, are evident in much of the world.

Against this background, this book not only asks the right questions but also proposes a way forward to a new era of enlightened public policy. That policy must be based on responsible wealth creation that accelerates economic growth, particularly in developing countries, but in an environmentally and socially responsible manner. As a result of such a policy, 2050 could be the time when the dream of a world free of poverty becomes a reality.

But if we choose other options and priorities, 2050 could be a time of social conflict and environmental degradation. This risk is a particular concern if today's income distribution, in which 80 percent of the world's population earns only 20 percent of the world's income, is not made more equal.

Economic growth could quadruple the size of the world economy by 2050, adding more than US$100 trillion to the world's gross domestic product. A giant economy of US$135 trillion poses new challenges. This growth will have major consequences for both production and consumption, particularly of food, water, and energy. This book asks us to face some hard truths, which are explored in detail in different chapters.

Agriculture and rural development can provide a substantial boost to the economies of poor countries and can contribute to lifting more than a billion people in rural areas out of extreme poverty. But if the rich world continues to hide behind harmful subsidies and trade restrictions, the growth potential of developing countries will not be realized. And if we continue to exclude the poor and disenfranchised from playing their rightful roles in society, social conflict may undermine the consensus needed for progress.

Responsible growth concerns more than economics, more than social development, more than environmental stewardship. It is an integrated approach, built on the moral imperative of protecting our planet and making it safe, secure, and prosperous for all. This goal can be achieved. But it will require foresight—and an unwavering commitment to combating world poverty.

James D. Wolfensohn
President
World Bank Group

PREFACE

This volume builds on the consensus developed at the August 2002 Johannesburg World Summit on Sustainable Development. It draws on the effort to achieve the Millennium Development Goals by 2015. And it looks beyond, to 2050, to envision a future that is far more prosperous and more equitable than today. This work raises some hard questions: How do we ensure that the progress achieved by 2015 is sustainable? What quality of growth will be required to attain this vision?

It is generally accepted that the Johannesburg Summit provided space for a broad dialogue on long-term sustainability, global equity, and justice and on the centrality of poverty reduction to sustainable development. Large United Nations meetings are sometimes criticized for their lack of concrete outputs. However, their lasting importance is often felt over the longer term in strategic choices, new and emerging priorities, and new modalities of implementation. Summits may also contribute to defining the big issues and big ideas for a certain period of time.

Long-term thinking is essential in dealing with sustainability issues (economic change, ecological threats). A consensus has emerged about the need to move toward a new development path, one that integrates economic growth with environmental responsibility and social equity. The World Bank has been advocating this vision of *responsible growth*, together with the concept that poverty reduction is not just an end in itself but also a precondition for peaceful coexistence and ecological survival.

Two years after the Johannesburg Summit, the vibrant interaction among governments, international organizations, civil society, and the private sector has continued and is here to stay. New multistakeholder coalitions are on the rise and, when supported by enlightened public policy, may become a powerful force for change. A responsible and accountable private sector and proactive civil society organizations are recognized to be central players in this process.

This volume does not aim to present a new paradigm, a new universal prescription. It builds on recent development thinking as embodied, in particular, in the sector strategy papers endorsed by the Board of Directors of the World Bank. The long-term vision of 2050, presented in chapter 1, is only one of many possible outcomes for the next decades. But the process of thinking about the long term forces us to start now to ask the right questions about development.

Ian Johnson
Vice President for Sustainable Development
World Bank

ACKNOWLEDGMENTS

This book is the result of a collaborative effort within the World Bank across a range of sectors and themes. It builds on analytical work, sector strategy papers, and position papers produced over the past two years. This publication, coordinated by Sergio Jellinek and Kirk Hamilton, has been prepared under the guidance of Ian Johnson and with contributions from Kevin Cleaver, Sushma Ganguly, John Briscoe, Csaba Csaki, and Ariel Dinar (Agriculture and Rural Department); Bernard Hoekman, Denis Medvedev, and Richard Newfarmer (Development Prospects Group and Development Research Group); Jamal Saghir, Elizabeth Kelley, Gary Stuggins, Kyran O'Sullivan, and Meike Van Ginneken (Energy and Water Department); Warren Evans, Kirk Hamilton, Todd Johnson, and Ede Jorge Ijjasz-Vasquez (Environment Department); James Douglas and David Cassells (Forest Team, Environment and Agriculture and Rural Development Departments); Steen Jorgensen, Robert Chase, and Rita Hilton (Social Development Department and Environmentally and Socially Sustainable Development Vice Presidency). Robert Watson of the Environmentally and Socially Sustainable Development Vice Presidency provided valuable reviews and inputs. Editorial services were provided by Communications Development Inc. and Publications Professionals LLC.

Odin Knudsen
Senior Adviser
Environmentally and Socially Sustainable Development
  Vice Presidency
World Bank

ABBREVIATIONS AND ACRONYMS

CO_2	Carbon dioxide
FDI	Foreign direct investment
GATS	General Agreement on Trade in Services
GDP	Gross domestic product
GEF	Global Environment Facility
GEMS/Air	Global Environment Monitoring System for air quality
NGO	Nongovernmental organization
OECD	Organisation for Economic Co-operation and Development
PRODEPINE	Development project of the Indigenous and Afro-Ecuadorian Pueblos
R&D	Research and development
SMART	Simple Moral Accountable Responsive Transparent
WTO	World Trade Organization

CHAPTER 1

RESPONSIBLE GROWTH
FOR THE NEW MILLENNIUM

G rowth is essential to reducing poverty and to reaching the Millennium Development Goals by 2015. But growth at any cost is not sustainable. Responsible growth is needed to sustain the coming increases in human welfare—in consumption, in health, in human skills, in social equity.

Consider a vision of the world of 2050. The world population could be 9 billion, up from 6 billion today (figure 1.1). Almost all that increase will show up in the cities and towns of developing countries. With growth of 2 percent per capita gross domestic product (GDP) in rich countries (the average over the past 20 years) and 3.3 percent in low- and middle-income countries (an optimistic figure, representing the growth experienced in the 1960s and 1970s), world income would be more than US$135 trillion, up from US$35 trillion today. With these growth rates to 2050, 40 percent of world income would be in low- and middle-income countries, twice their share of 20 percent today (figure 1.2).

With per capita incomes in low- and middle-income countries rising at 3.3 percent a year from today, the average income in these countries would be US$6,300 by 2050.[1] Basic human needs for shelter, food, and clothing could be more than met. And people would be healthier and more skilled. Even pessimistic estimates place life expectancy in today's low- and middle-income countries at 72 years

---

This chapter builds on "Johannesburg and Beyond: An Agenda for Action" (World Bank 2002) and was prepared by Kirk Hamilton, with the contributions and guidance of Ian Johnson.

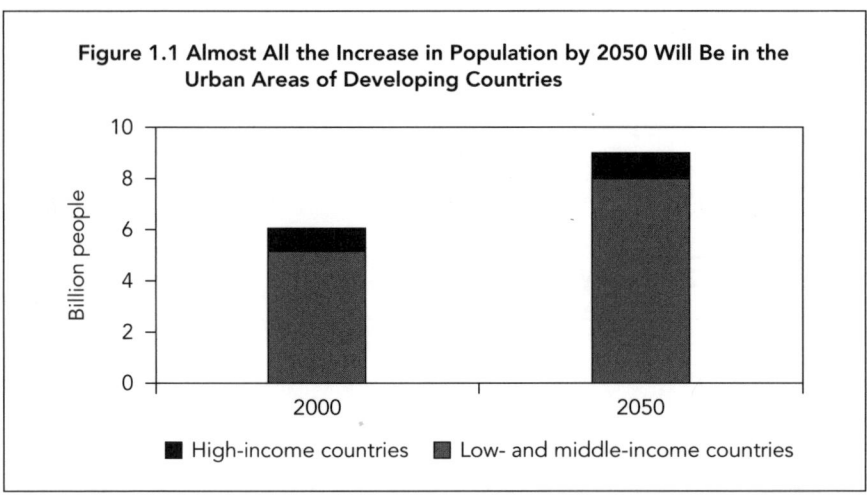

Figure 1.1 Almost All the Increase in Population by 2050 Will Be in the Urban Areas of Developing Countries

Source: World Bank 2001 and authors' estimates.

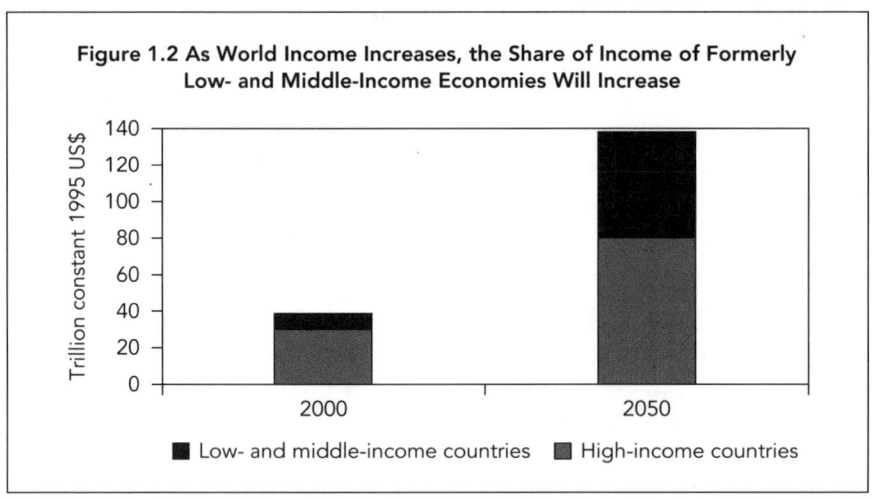

Figure 1.2 As World Income Increases, the Share of Income of Formerly Low- and Middle-Income Economies Will Increase

Source: World Bank 2001 and authors' estimates.

(up from 64 years today) and under-5 mortality at 17 per 1,000 live births (down from 85 per 1,000 today). Adult illiteracy rates could be less than 5 percent, a fifth of today's 25 percent.

In 2050, more than 65 percent of the population will live in urban areas. Infrastructure and housing needs, if city dwellers are to enjoy healthy and productive lives, will be huge. But this demand also presents a great opportunity. Because most of these infrastructure and housing investments have yet to be designed, they could be made to contribute to environmentally sustainable urban environments.

If present trends continue, the world of 2050 will also be much less biologically diverse. Part of the challenge is to reduce the number of poor communities dependent on fragile ecosystems. Particularly important is finding the financing to preserve biodiversity, both through protective expenditures and through compensation to communities that may have to restrict their exploitation of natural areas, for the benefit of their countries and the world as a whole. Ecotourism can help pay for preservation, as can new approaches such as systems of payments for environmental services.

The nature of growth in the rich world is also an issue. Today, 80 percent of global GDP goes to only 20 percent of the world's people. Consumption patterns for energy, water, food, manufactured goods, and services are highly skewed and will remain so for the near future. Are those patterns sustainable? Probably not, for as incomes in developing countries grow, consumption will increase to meet their development aspirations.

A world with US$135 trillion in GDP simply cannot rely on current production and consumption patterns. If subsidies, mispricing, and inadequate taxation of environmentally damaging products continue to provide the wrong incentives for consumers and producers in the rich world, and if the developing world continues to grow wealthier, we can expect great damage to the environment and its ability to sustain growth. A major transformation, starting in the rich world, will be needed to decouple growth and environmental impacts and to radically change the composition of the world's output toward high input efficiency and environmental responsibility. Future global patterns of consumption and production must become a part of the global public policy dialogue.

This chapter examines the drivers of growth—agriculture, trade, energy, water, innovation, human development, and social development. It also considers the challenges and constraints. What are the possible consequences of a much larger scale of human activity? Thinking about the long term can pinpoint some of the critical decisions that must be taken soon to prevent undesirable outcomes much later.

ACHIEVING RESPONSIBLE GROWTH

At the assumed growth rates, the total GDP of developing countries in 2050 will be twice that of industrial countries today. This change raises some stark questions: How resource intensive will these economies be? How energy and carbon intensive? How pollution intensive?

We can draw some tentative conclusions by looking across industrial and developing countries today. Economies restructure as they grow, with most growth occurring in service sectors, which are less harmful to the environment. Services could constitute 60 percent of GDP in developing countries in 2050, but that figure would still be 10 percentage points lower than in industrial countries today. It is therefore possible that primary and industrial sectors will have a significant weight in the economies of developing countries.

Vehicle ownership also has strong environmental links. The assumed income growth could entail a quadrupling of vehicles in developing countries. The potential increase in vehicle emissions could be mitigated by the increasing proportion of newer vehicles in the fleet, by better technology, and by better maintenance.

Higher incomes will almost certainly reduce pressure on local biomass as an energy source. But the energy substituted may be carbon intensive; historically, each 1 percent increase in GDP has led to a 1 percent increase in carbon dioxide (CO_2) emissions. Technical progress and structural change can make a difference, however. From 1980 to 1996, the average CO_2 emitted per dollar of world GDP fell by 12.5 percent.

Many decisions in the near term will have long-term consequences. Much of the infrastructure built in the next 20 years will still be with us in 2050. Perhaps more important, some choices are irreversible or can be reversed only with great difficulty. Species loss is the canonical example. And CO_2, once emitted, has an atmospheric adjustment time of more than 100 years. Climate change will reduce the quantity and quality of water in most arid and semiarid regions in addition to increasing the frequency of floods and droughts worldwide. It will decrease agricultural productivity throughout the tropics and subtropics for almost any degree of warming, it will increase the incidence of vector- and waterborne diseases and heat stress

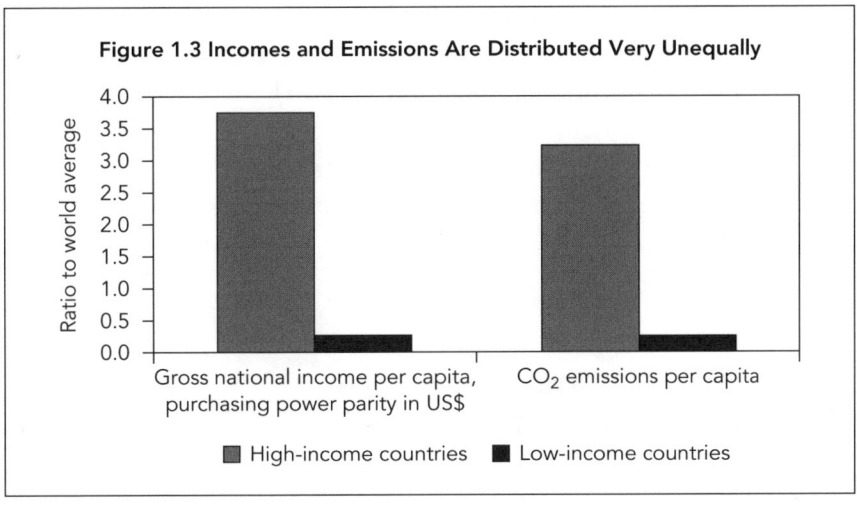

Figure 1.3 Incomes and Emissions Are Distributed Very Unequally

Ratio to world average

Gross national income per capita, purchasing power parity in US$ — CO_2 emissions per capita

■ High-income countries ■ Low-income countries

Source: World Bank 2001.

mortality, it will make hydropower less reliable in some regions, and it will adversely affect biodiversity at the species and ecosystem levels.

Incomes and pressures on the global environment are now distributed very unequally (figure 1.3). Poor countries suffer four times the incidence of environmental disease observed in rich countries. Dealing with indoor air pollution and hygienic practices could have a major effect on the global burden of disease. Poor people have little voice in the decisions that affect them. Poor households depend on the quality of local natural resources for their livelihood. Poor countries and poor households are inordinately at risk from natural disasters. Small island states, South Asian countries, and Sub-Saharan Africa are particularly vulnerable to global climate change.

Meeting the Millennium Development Targets for 2015 is an essential step on the road to a prosperous and sustainable world and potentially the basis for a virtuous cycle of growth and human development in the poor nations of the world. Faster growth is the key to meeting the targets, and the payoffs will be great. Faster growth means less extreme poverty, less child malnutrition, and faster progress on many of the other Millennium Development Goals. But the benefits of that growth must be widely spread, and it must be environmentally and socially responsible.

What will it take for such steady gains in income to materialize? Macroeconomic stability will need to be sustained. Massive infrastructure will have to be financed and built, with investment expenditures in developing countries rising from today's US$200 billion a year to nearly US$1.5 trillion in 2050. Human capital, in terms of both knowledge and health, will have to be invested in and maintained. And technological progress will be required across a whole range of sectors.

ACTING NOW TO LAY THE FOUNDATION FOR A SUSTAINABLE FUTURE

Growing to a world economy of nearly US$135 trillion poses enormous risks to the natural environment, and the risks are greatest in developing countries. Investment decisions in the near future must factor in those risks and provide some insurance against undesirable surprises. Some of the most difficult issues will involve tradeoffs between preserving natural systems and pressing forward with development. Truly global issues will require collective action on an unprecedented scale. Meeting those challenges will demand sound management of the many capital assets underpinning development:

- Investing in *physical capital* in buildings, machines, and infrastructure
- Managing *natural capital*, including the investment of the rents from exhaustible resources
- Building up health and *human capital*
- Sustaining and building the *social capital* that supports both welfare and productive activities
- Investing in *intellectual capital*, the new knowledge and technology that can foster increases in productivity
- Channeling *financial capital* to its most productive uses, while accounting for environmental and social spillovers

Actions must also be taken in this decade to lay the foundations that will carry us well into the middle of this century. Global and national policies, investment strategies, and new institutional relationships will need to be developed. In today's interconnected world, the management of fragile ecosystems, transboundary water systems, communicable disease, climate change, and scientific and technological pathways and knowledge systems all warrant attention. Management of these systems will require cooperative action and new institutional relationships. In today's mobile world, issues of demographic change, migration, and social conflict need to be addressed. This fact suggests greater attention to promoting the long-term development of social and human capital.

Sustained growth is the key to realizing a world without poverty by mid-century. What will fuel this growth, and what will support it? The starting point for many developing countries, given the concentration of poverty in rural areas and the share of agriculture in GDP, must be rural development and growth in agricultural production. For all countries, investments in human capital, including health, will be essential. But this growth and development depends, in turn, on critical inputs, particularly water and energy. And agricultural technology must feed a growing world and ensure that this growth is sustained—and responsible.

Supplying energy, water, and sanitation, not to mention transport and communications, will require major infrastructure investments. It is increasingly clear that investments in electricity, water supply, and sanitation underpin not only growth in incomes but growth in healthfulness and reductions in mortality as well, particularly for children under the age of 5 years.

Acting now also means making progress on the "aid and trade" agenda. Development assistance, partnered with good governance in recipient countries, can be a powerful engine for growth. But research suggests that the benefits from expanding trade by reducing the trade barriers faced by developing countries could dwarf development assistance. By 2015, annual income gains from expanded trade could equal US$350 billion in developing countries (compared with current aid flows of roughly US$50 billion), while increasing incomes in rich countries by US$170 billion.

Trade can thus be a powerful engine of sustainable economic growth and poverty reduction. But the relationship between trade and growth is complex and not automatic. A trade minister cannot simply pull the lever labeled "improved trade policy" and expect that trade will boom, economic growth will accelerate, and the poor will

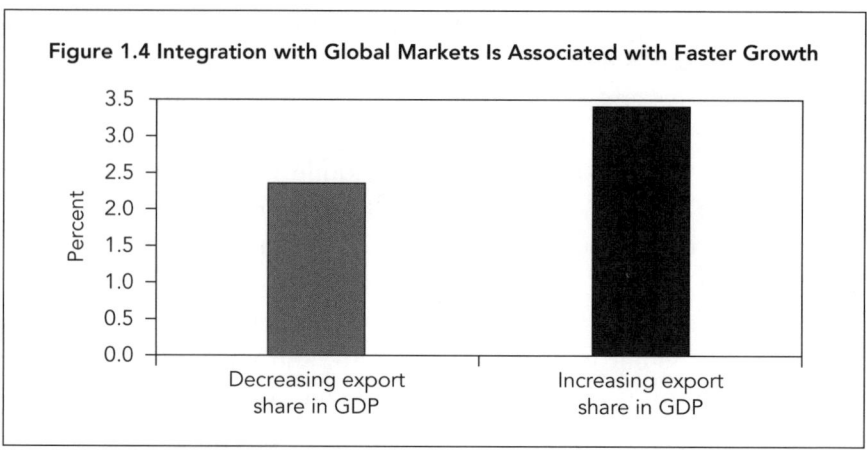

Figure 1.4 Integration with Global Markets Is Associated with Faster Growth

Source: World Bank 2003.

benefit. Instead, governments everywhere have to pursue a mix of policies to get the trade engine running smoothly. The international community—rich and poor countries working together—can use trade agreements (the Doha negotiations in particular) to improve their trade policies, support the implementation of complementary policies, and create new opportunities for developing countries.

Greater trade integration is associated with faster growth (figure 1.4).[2] That said, the links from specific trade policy instruments to trade outcomes and growth are less clear, and controversy over causality abounds. The lesson from the analyses swirling around those controversies is that trade policy can help promote and sustain growth, but it requires complementary measures to realize its full potential.

ACHIEVING SUSTAINABLE AGRICULTURE AND RURAL DEVELOPMENT

Rural development and agriculture are linked to the Millennium Development Goals through several mechanisms. The first is hunger—specifically malnutrition of children under 5 years of age. To reduce hunger, food production in low-income countries needs to continue to grow faster than the population grows. Since 1970, food production in low-income countries has outpaced population growth—except in Sub-Saharan Africa, where technology has lagged and population growth has exceeded productivity growth. With rising incomes and population growth, the demand for food could double by 2050. Higher incomes will shift the pattern of demand toward higher-protein foods, with consequences for fisheries, aquaculture, and livestock husbandry. Food will likely be a continuing problem in Sub-Saharan Africa and in some of the lowest-income countries in Latin America and Asia. What is required? More focused efforts to expand food production in the lowest-income countries, especially in Sub-Saharan Africa.

Agricultural growth is also essential to income growth in most low-income countries, because agricultural output constitutes such a large percentage of total output (for all low-income countries, 24 percent of total output comes from agriculture). Agriculture also provides a safety net for the poor, both rural and urban.

But sustained agricultural growth cannot occur by increasing the area under cultivation. Further expansion of arable land would be on marginal land, at high cost to the biodiversity we have left. Environmentally responsible agricultural growth must focus on intensifying cultivation on land already farmed and on expanding infrastructure in rural areas.

Because the best food-producing land is already used, raising the productivity of land and other inputs is the key to boosting output. Past increases in agricultural productivity have been impressive. From 1980 to 1996, the value of food production increased by 57 percent, while the population grew by 31 percent. The scope for improvements in low-income countries is large. The cereal yield in Europe, at 5.2 metric tons per hectare, is 2.8 times that in low-income countries. Cereal yields in East Asia are three times those in Sub-Saharan Africa. Limits on the agricultural potential of some regions mean that those gaps cannot be closed completely, but the potential to narrow them is substantial.

Achieving the productivity gains needed requires an agricultural revolution for the drylands. Sustaining agriculture will require close attention to land and water degradation, nutrient management, integrated pest management, conservation, and the policies and institutions that can engender better practice. Adapting to climate change is another key priority.

New agricultural technologies will drive this growth, but technology alone cannot do the job. Agricultural growth also requires better markets for agricultural products, better infrastructure (especially rural roads), better rural financial services, and better policies, phasing out the ones that discriminate heavily against agriculture.

ATTAINING SUSTAINABLE ENERGY

Energy output has to grow, and the quality of energy used in poor countries will have to change. Cleaner stoves, cleaner fuels, and better indoor ventilation will reduce indoor air pollution and improve health. But a world economy of US$135 trillion will demand much more energy for industry and for small and medium-size enterprises—and for moving households up the energy ladder, from traditional fuels to a combination of kerosene and bottled gas and, ultimately, to electricity for selective uses. For electricity alone, investment requirements of US$3.5 trillion in developing countries can be foreseen to 2030.

Today 1.6 billion people lack access to electricity, and 2.4 billion rely on traditional biomass for cooking and heating. Today the richest 20 percent of the world's population consumes 58 percent of total energy, while the poorest 20 percent consumes only 4 percent.

Electricity in the home is clean, reducing health risks (indoor air is estimated to kill 2.5 million women and children a year). It also enables refrigeration, modern communications, and more time for reading and income-earning activities (by providing light in the evening). Electricity in the workplace is needed for the jobs that raise the incomes of the poor; electricity in the community is needed for health clinics and schools.

Given the potential quadrupling of energy use by 2050, the world must become radically less carbon intensive to avoid environmental disasters and health disasters. Essential for this change are significant increases in the use of renewables and low-carbon alternatives for industry, homes, and transportation and significant gains in energy efficiency, both through better application of current technologies and through new technologies. Improvements so far, while important, help only at the margin. From 1961 to 1975, each 1 percent rise in income in member countries of the Organisation for Economic Co-operation and

Development entailed a 1.44 percent rise is electricity generation; from 1976 to 1998, this figure fell to 1 percent. And carbon intensity decreased: from 1980 to 1996, the average CO_2 emitted per constant U.S. dollar of world GDP fell by 12.5 percent, despite massive increases in coal burning in China and India. But the reduction in carbon intensity still leaves today's world operating beyond its carbon-absorptive capacity, thus presenting a major challenge for future growth.

The low energy consumption in poor countries (especially of electricity) suggests that energy consumption will grow at least as fast as GDP, and electricity consumption will grow even faster. If so, an additional 15 million megawatts of new electricity capacity will be required by 2050. The equivalent of 1,000 large electric power plants would have to be built annually to meet that need. Does this growth represent an environmental threat? With current fossil fuel technology, yes. But because this capacity has yet to be planned and built, there is a huge opportunity to move to a sustainable energy pathway, if poor countries have access to new energy technologies.

Dealing with energy subsidies is a major part of the agenda. Electricity subsidies are nominally aimed at the poor, who have little or no access. Reducing and retargeting subsidies, while providing access and lifeline rates to poor households, will increase efficiency gains and the sustainability of power.

REALIZING SUSTAINABLE WATER

Water cuts across many of the challenges in health, welfare, agriculture, and energy. Some rivers no longer reach the sea. Half the world's wetlands disappeared in the past century. A fifth of freshwater fish are extinct or endangered. Subsoil water is being mined, and many aquifers are turning salty. The World Commission on Water estimates that water use will increase by 50 percent in the next 30 years—and that half the world's people, largely in the developing regions of Africa, the Middle East, and South Asia, will be under severe water stress by 2025.

Today's water sources are being degraded by assaults on upper watersheds, the depletion of aquifers, and the pollution of groundwater and surface water. Meeting water needs will require substantial improvements in the management of water sources. Inappropriate pricing policies have led to massive waste and have not provided benefits to the poor, because the poor often lack access to water connections. Many developing countries need to make large investments in water infrastructure at all levels.

Developing water infrastructure is essential in many developing countries to generate wealth, mitigate risk, and alleviate poverty. This development must be done with more attention to the environment and more equitable sharing of benefits and costs.

Delivering water to farmers, industry, and households, while maintaining water's ecological function, will present major challenges. Managing water across subnational regions and across national boundaries will grow in importance. Institutional frameworks and management instruments, including pricing and regulatory reform, will be required.

The agenda for irrigation (which takes 70 percent of the fresh water used each year) includes moving from expansion and construction to intensification and better demand management. Key priorities include increasing the productivity of water and infrastructure; developing a realistic, sequenced approach to cost recovery; scaling up the remarkably successful water user associations; and reforming the formal irrigation institutions, including the participation of the private sector. Investments in research and development must also be supported to reduce water consumption in water-intensive crops.

Poor households can have safe, affordable water and sanitation if costs are reduced and alternative service providers are encouraged. In urban areas, that means targeting subsidies to the poorest, permitting competition in delivery, and structuring contracts and regulatory incentives to facilitate extension of services to poor communities. In small towns and rural areas, that means empowering communities to choose their service levels and service delivery mechanisms, vesting them with ownership rights and the authority to choose service providers, and establishing financial policies and instruments that encourage them to contribute to capital costs and to pay for all operation and maintenance costs. Incorporating the views of women is particularly important in making these choices, because water provision often falls to women in many developing countries.

Focusing on health outcomes suggests that quantity of water, as well as quality, is a critical issue for poor households. Hygienic uses of water, such as hand washing, are more frequent when enough water—beyond basic drinking and cooking needs—is available.

Climate change is expected to increase the frequency of droughts and floods. This increase will pose an additional challenge for flood control, which will remain largely a responsibility of the public sector.

SUSTAINING TECHNOLOGY

Technology also cuts across all paths to the future. Developments in energy and agriculture will be particularly critical. The carriers of technological knowledge are mostly private enterprises, but the public sector has to encourage innovation and technological diffusion. A clear, transparent, and well-enforced framework for intellectual property rights, contract law, and financial regulations is important in creating the right incentives for technology to thrive.

For Energy

There are promising developments in energy production off the grid, which are particularly important for rural areas of developing countries. Small hydro, geothermal, biomass, wind, and solar technologies are becoming more competitive per kilowatt-hour. They are also climate friendly. For large centralized systems, gas turbine and cleaner coal technologies offer greater cost-effectiveness and lower pollution intensities.

Decisions about centralized versus decentralized energy systems will have other important effects. Capital-intensive centralized systems tend to be natural monopolies and not good for efficiency. The large scale and long service lives of centralized systems mean that countries will be living with the consequences of investment decisions for decades—making development outcomes highly path dependent.

Biomass will continue to be an important energy source for the poorest households in developing countries, at least until 2030. A key goal must, therefore, be the development and use of biomass fuel technologies that are clean and efficient.

For Agriculture

Three trends in agricultural technology could greatly affect food availability. First, new developments in the biological sciences can increase the yield and quality of food and fiber, can permit food production in unfavorable areas, and can offer scope for intensification, thus reducing pressure on natural areas. Second, better farming systems can apply knowledge of both crop physiology and crop ecology—for example, integrated pest management and minimum tillage. Third, multidisciplinary and multistakeholder approaches to agricultural research can enable subsistence farmers to participate in variety breeding programs and to use rural technologies applicable to their needs.

It is clear that technology policy—protection of intellectual property, tax treatment of research and development, investment in basic science—can have an important effect on economic growth and efficiency. But the technological paths chosen must be environmentally and socially responsible.

SUSTAINING SOCIETIES

Building Human Capital

A key step in building human capital will be the attainment of universal primary education—the completion, by all children, of 5 to 6 years of primary education. That means that more than 112 million children, age 5 to 11 years, will need to be drawn into primary school now, and those enrollment rates must be sustained as the population grows in the future. With young girls accounting for more than two-thirds of children out of school, special efforts will need to be made to ensure that they complete the primary cycle. The contribution of education to development is significant. Increased education is central to the adoption of new technologies and environmentally sound practices. It also contributes to slower population growth, lower mortality rates, and better health and well-being of children. It can also be an important tool in helping limit the spread of HIV/AIDS.

Education and the management of knowledge will underpin long-term sustained growth well into this century. Taking action to meet the Millennium Development Goals for education is a priority, but so too is building the long-term educational and knowledge systems for future generations.

Improving health implies both (a) delivering health care services to reduce the direct causes of ill health and death and (b) addressing the underlying causes of ill health through prevention. Recent estimates suggest that an additional 0.1 percent of the GDP of rich countries could deliver quality health care services in the developing world. In prevention, the environmental dimension is increasingly prominent, particularly for children under the age of 5. About a fifth of the burden of disease in developing countries is linked to environmental conditions, including insufficient and unsafe water, lack of sanitation, uncontrolled disease vectors (such as mosquitoes), and indoor and outdoor air pollution. Dealing with the environmental causes of death and disease is highly cost-effective, and it yields other benefits, including reduced time spent fetching water.

HIV/AIDS is a major destroyer of human capital in Sub-Saharan Africa and other parts of the world. Estimates of its economic impact in Africa suggest annual GDP growth reductions of 0.3 percent to 1.5 percent. But some argue that the impact would be much higher if the effects on school attendance of AIDS orphans and children from single-parent families were taken into account. Access to affordable AIDS treatments and continuing efforts toward a cure are keys to maintaining and building human capital in AIDS-affected countries.

Building on Social Development and Social Capital

Responsible growth must be built on both social development and social capital. The key principles to ensure that development is socially responsible are inclusion, cohesion, and accountability:

- *Inclusive societies* promote equal access to opportunities. To this end, societies must alter formal and informal rules that limit the capabilities of the disempowered and encourage the participation of diverse individuals and groups in development activities.

- *Cohesive societies* are willing and able to work together to address common needs, overcome constraints, and consider diverse interests. They resolve differences in a civil, nonconfrontational way that promotes peace and security.
- *Accountable institutions* are transparent and serve the public interest in an effective, efficient, and fair way. They respond to people's needs. Accountability is the obligation of those who can exercise political, economic, or other forms of power to account for, and take responsibility for, their actions.

Like human capital, social capital—the institutions, relationships, and norms that shape the quality and quantity of a society's social interactions—is essential to sustainable reduction of poverty. Social capital can have a major effect on the income and well-being of the poor by improving the effectiveness of development programs. How? Through higher productivity; through better management of common resources; and through greater access of poor households to water, sanitation, credit, and education in rural and urban areas. That is why we need to understand how best to invest in social capital and to prevent its erosion through social conflict.

Dealing with Inequality in the Near Term

The picture here suggests a more equitable world in 2050. But the stresses that current levels of inequality are placing on the international order cannot be ignored. The "aid and trade" agenda is critical in the near term. Providing the development financing to meet the Millennium Development Goals and opening markets in rich countries to the products of developing countries can reduce the current extremes of inequality across nations—and the social and political consequences of that inequality.

Improving Governance and Rule of Law in Developing Countries

Better governance is widely recognized as an essential part of the global deal between rich and poor. The potential benefits in developing countries are enormous. Better governance will lead to greater social equity in developing countries, will increase the effectiveness of public investments, and will open the floodgates for private investment—but ensuring environmentally and socially responsible investment will be key.

Providing Public Goods

Technological optimism is part of the vision for 2050. Maintaining 3.3 percent per capita growth in poor countries will require big productivity gains. But it is important to emphasize that there are major issues of public goods in research and development, particularly for agricultural technologies and treatments for infectious diseases. Financiers of the rich world cannot invest profitably in tropical agricultural technology or treatments for malaria, but the gains in social welfare from doing so will be large. We need a more effective and consistent approach to financing investment in technological public goods.

Managing Migration

Will the relatively low rates of migration from poor to rich countries continue? The demographic situation of many rich countries, particularly Japan and countries in Western Europe, will deteriorate rapidly in the next decades. Germany, Italy, Japan, and the Netherlands will have elderly dependency ratios of 45 to 49 percent by 2030. This shift not only implies less dynamic societies; it also foretells major fiscal inequities. Generational accounting suggests that cuts in transfer payments of 40 percent in Italy, more than 25 percent in Japan, and 20 percent in the United States will be required to bring intergenerational transfers—primarily public pension and health care schemes—into line with government budget constraints. Opening those countries to more immigration, by rebalancing the population structure, could help relieve this fiscal stress.

CREATING STRONGER PARTNERSHIPS
FOR A SUSTAINABLE WORLD

The Monterrey Summit on Finance for Development laid the basis for a new development partnership. That partnership was based on a framework of mutual accountability between industrial and developing countries. Developing countries acknowledged that they must take responsibility for good governance and sound policies, as African leaders are doing under the New Partnership for Africa's Development. Industrial countries committed to ensuring that aid resources match progress on policy reforms, to tearing down trade barriers that harm the poorest, to implementing the Heavily In-debted Poor Countries Initiative, and to building capacity using the power of the knowledge economy. Funding action to achieve and measure the Millennium Development Goals is the starting point, and the extra 0.2 percent of annual GDP in rich countries that this funding will require is modest by any measure.

The Doha Round of trade agreements was to be a development round, which required industrial countries to open their markets to ensure that all countries—especially the poorest—could enjoy the benefits of trade. However, the ministerial meeting in Cancún and subsequent attempts to revitalize the stalled negotiations have not produced the expected results.

But there are some bright spots. The Global Environment Facility (GEF) is responding to the obligation of the industrial countries to ad-dress biodiversity loss, climate change, and international water degra-dation. Very often the costs for a poor country to conserve resources of global importance exceed the benefits to the country; at the same time, the sum of local and global benefits may exceed the costs. The GEF fills a critical financing gap. As threats to biodiversity in particular mount, expanding funding for the GEF must be a priority, along with developing systems of payments for environmental services and ex-tending efforts to integrate biodiversity into the productive landscape.

The Montreal Protocol on Substances that Deplete the Ozone Layer represents a major success story of multilateral action. Coming into force in 1990, the protocol commits both industrial and develop-ing countries to eliminating the use of ozone-depleting substances and provides multilateral funding to support the phase-out of those substances in developing countries. From 1986 to 2000, the consump-tion of ozone-depleting substances dropped from 1.1 million metric tons a year to fewer than 100,000, and the program is on track for complete elimination by 2010. Without the Montreal Protocol, levels of ozone-depleting substances in the atmosphere would have increased tenfold by 2050, which could have led to up to 20 million more cases of skin cancer and 130 million more cases of eye cataracts than occurred in 1980. The protocol is one of the most successful international environmental agreements ever.

Public-private partnerships have become more relevant. Financial resources from the private sector are key to the supply of many goods and services, including water and electricity, that have traditionally been in the public sector. But we need to recognize that the private sector on its own cannot deliver public goods. Public and private sectors must each play their particular roles in the development process.

We also need to track progress. Doing so will require North-South partnerships on the adoption of agreed indicators—for transparent tracking of development progress in rich nations and poor. Ideally, those indicators should marry the economic, social, and environmental domains, since it is at this intersection that many of the issues relating to sustainability are key. Indicators can be controversial, because they highlight poor performance as well as good. Decision-makers must thus look beyond the controversy and use indicators to guide the policy choices for responsible growth.

The chapters that follow detail the challenges and opportunities in agriculture, trade, energy, water, sanitation, forests and environmental resources, and social development. They describe the actions that will be required to realize the vision of a more equitable and sustainable world in 2050.

NOTES

1. All dollar figures for projected GDP are constant 1995 U.S. dollars.
2. For contrasting views on the state of the evidence on trade, trade policies, and growth, see Srinivasan and Bhagwati (2000), Rodriguez and Rodrik (1999), and Bernanke and Rogoff (2001).

REFERENCES

Bernanke, Ben, and Kenneth Rogoff, eds. 2001. *Macroeconomics Annual 2001.* Cambridge, Mass.: MIT Press.

Rodriguez, Francisco, and Dani Rodrik. 1999. "Trade Policy and Economic Growth: A Skeptic's Guide to the Cross-National Evidence." NBER Working Paper 7081. National Bureau of Economic Research, Cambridge, Mass.

Srinivasan, T. N., and Jadgish Bhagwati. 2000. "Outward-Orientation and Development: Are Revisionists Right?" In *Macroeconomics Annual 2000*. Cambridge, Mass.: MIT Press.

World Bank. 2001. *World Development Indicators*. Washington, D.C.

_____. 2002. "Johannesburg and Beyond: An Agenda for Action." Washington, D.C. Processed.

_____. 2003. *Global Economic Prospects and the Developing Countries 2004: Realizing the Development Promise of the Doha Agenda*. Washington, D.C.

CHAPTER 2

AGRICULTURE AND RURAL DEVELOPMENT—PILLARS FOR GROWTH IN POOR COUNTRIES

Some global trends in agriculture and rural development are cause for concern:

- *Persistent rural poverty.* About 70 percent of the world's poor live in rural areas, and in the world's poorer regions, the majority of the population remains rural and is engaged in agricultural activities.
- *Significant urban-rural gap.* Rural areas still suffer more from extreme poverty, weak institutions, low public service delivery, and underdeveloped infrastructure.
- *Stagnating agricultural production with declines in production growth in low-income countries.* Despite its critical role in sustaining livelihoods, global agricultural production has stagnated in recent years, with some important regional variations (table 2.1).

There is, however, some encouraging news, if the environmental aspects are well managed:

- *Faster agricultural growth in Sub-Saharan Africa.* Agricultural productivity in Africa increased in the 1990s. This growth is attributable mainly to increases in crop productivity.

This chapter builds on the World Bank's Agriculture and Rural Development Strategy (World Bank 2003a) and was prepared by Kevin Cleaver, Sushma Ganguly, Csaba Csaki, and Ariel Dinar of the Agriculture and Rural Department.

Table 2.1 Agriculture Value Added Annual Growth Rates (percent)

Region	1990–99	2000–02
Eastern Asia and the Pacific	3.5	2.2
Europe and Central Asia	–2.5	2.4
Latin America and the Caribbean	2.6	2.1
Middle East and North Africa	3.2	3.4
South Asia	3.2	1.0
Sub-Saharan Africa	2.4	3.3
Low-income countries	2.8	1.8
Middle-income countries	2.2	2.3
High-income countries	1.1	2.3
World	1.9	2.0

Source: World Bank data.

- *A bigger role for livestock and high-value crops.* As global food consumption shifts from heavy dependence on grains to more animal products, livestock plays an increased role in meeting changing food demand. Another area of agricultural activity that holds promise for rural development is increased cultivation of high-value crops such as fresh fruits, flowers, vegetables, beans, and condiments. World prices for those products have performed better than prices for other traditional agricultural goods.
- *Promising new approaches.* Innovative approaches to rural development—such as community-driven development, community forestry, watershed management, and decentralized agriculture services—can be scaled up for significant effects.

Over the next 30 to 50 years, rural areas will have to feed an additional 2 billion to 3 billion people globally and will have to substantially improve the diets of the 2.5 billion to 3 billion people living on less than US$2 a day. Doing so will require tilting institutional rules to move assets into the hands of smallholders, reducing soil erosion, and adopting agricultural practices that restore soil fertility. It will also require sharing rural land and water to serve the expanding urban population and to meet environmental needs.

WORLDWIDE TRADE POLICY REFORM

Because so many of the poor derive their livelihoods from agriculture, developing countries have a huge stake in the full integration of agriculture under multilateral trade rules. A major reason for the limited growth of agricultural trade and for the inability of developing countries to enlarge their share of this trade is high protection in the large markets of the industrial world. High subsidies and other forms of trade protection impair the ability of developing countries to compete with farmers from the industrial world. They also encourage the sale of surpluses on world markets, thereby depressing world prices and undermining the potential contribution of agriculture to global prosperity.

The economic welfare benefits of global agricultural trade reform for the developing world are estimated at US$142 billion annually. For the developing countries, the impact of agricultural trade liberalization by the industrial countries alone would be more than 50 percent of the official development assistance given to developing countries in 2001 (figure 2.1). These countries are the developing world's largest potential market for agricultural products. Considering the potential for significant increases in income in developing countries from agricultural trade, it is crucial that the industrial

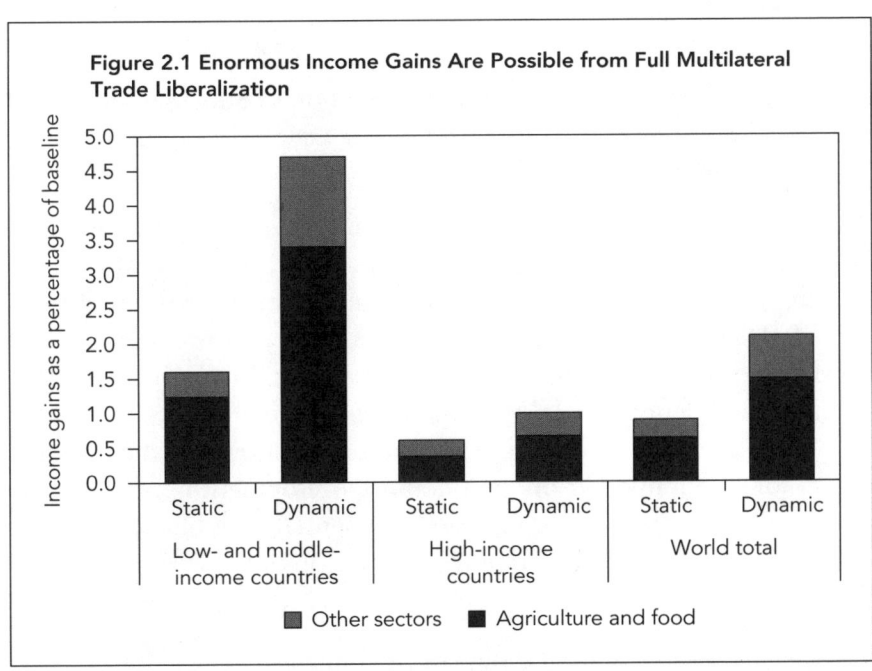

Figure 2.1 Enormous Income Gains Are Possible from Full Multilateral Trade Liberalization

Note: *Static gains* refer to results holding productivity constant. *Dynamic gains* allow productivity to respond to sector-specific export-to-output ratios.
Source: World Bank 2003b.

countries liberalize their agricultural markets by removing trade barriers to open market access for developing countries' products and by phasing out subsidies.

Developing countries will benefit by improving their own trade policies and by using the system of multilateral trade rules to expand their trade, thus enhancing their development prospects (see chapter 3). The broader development community can support better agricultural and trade policies through the following:

- Increasing advocacy of trade liberalization in both industrial and developing countries.
- Mainstreaming agricultural trade liberalization and trade capacity development.
- Facilitating capacity building through technical assistance and training on trade-related issues.
- Increasing assistance to developing countries in the area of standards and sanitary and phytosanitary regulations.
- Conducting analytical work at both global and country levels to identify key areas for future policy reform.

Liberalization of Market Access and Reduction of Subsidies in Member Countries of the Organisation for Economic Co-operation and Development

A genuine reform of trade policies and liberalization in the member countries of the Organisation for Economic Co-operation and Development is a precondition for unleashing the agricultural potential of the developing world and for significantly reducing rural poverty worldwide (figure 2.2). But the ongoing World Trade Organization negotiations reveal the difficulties of the process.

The trade policy reforms in the member countries of the Organisation for Economic Co-operation and Development need to follow the lines of the progressive proposals presented by a bloc of middle-income countries at the current negotiations of the World Trade Organization:

- Market access should be significantly improved.
- Export credits and subsidies should be fully eliminated.

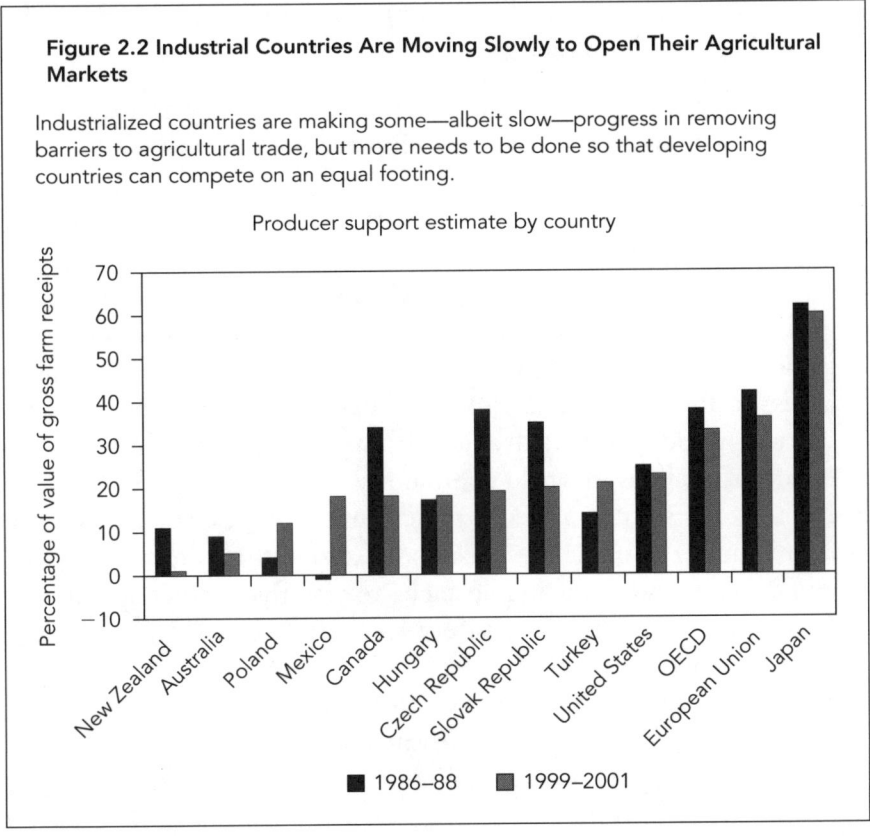

Figure 2.2 Industrial Countries Are Moving Slowly to Open Their Agricultural Markets

Industrialized countries are making some—albeit slow—progress in removing barriers to agricultural trade, but more needs to be done so that developing countries can compete on an equal footing.

Producer support estimate by country

Source: OECD 2002.

• Concerns of developing countries should be properly addressed.
• Nontrade concerns should be handled adequately.

Sound Policy Environments in Developing Countries

The developing countries also have work to do if they want to gain long-run benefits from trade liberalization. Their domestic policies must allow domestic producers to respond to changing domestic and foreign conditions. Developing countries should be supported in their efforts to improve their own policy environments for rural development and thereby enhance their development prospects. The nature and degree of the reforms will be influenced by the extent of agricultural trade and subsidy reform in the industrial countries. The focus will be on the following:

- Improving the macroeconomic framework for agricultural and rural growth by correcting remaining biases in the macroeconomic environment.
- Espousing the principles of nondiscriminatory taxation and reform credibility in both theory and practice.
- Supporting an enabling policy environment for agricultural trade and market access (a) by reducing trade barriers and antiexport bias in order to promote growth in agricultural trade, (b) by widening access to foreign markets, (c) by reducing protection for nonagricultural goods, and (d) by developing policies to minimize the effects of declines in world commodity prices on farmers.
- Introducing sound food and agricultural policies; supporting the development of effective markets for agricultural inputs, outputs, and services; and removing obstacles to effective market operations.
- Designing and targeting safety nets that directly protect the poor—particularly rural dwellers.
- Assisting in the establishment of complementary legal and regulatory frameworks that support private enterprises.
- Improving the operation of land markets and land administration, promoting land reform for countries with inequitable land distribution, and promoting equal access to secure landholding, especially by women.

Good Governance and Good Institutions

Good governance and good institutions are indispensable for sound rural development. The overcentralized institutional structures that are characteristic of many government administrative systems also sap the effectiveness of development investments and policies.

Decentralization offers great scope for improving delivery of public sector functions. Facilitating further decentralization in rural areas is an important part of the policy agenda. With decentralization, local governments must be given sufficient fiscal resources to discharge their new responsibilities. Political decentralization is also necessary, because it promotes accountability and governance reforms at the local level.

Governments should be encouraged to concentrate on providing public goods; on establishing legal, administrative, and regulatory systems that correct for market failures; on facilitating efficient operation of the private sector; and on protecting the interests of the disadvantaged. A set of priorities to promote the development of effective institutions for rural development has emerged:

- Strengthen local administrative capacity.
- Transfer responsibility for services to the administrative level closest to the users.
- Enhance the accountability for public administration at every level.
- Adopt participatory approaches, including increased political space and participation in decisionmaking bodies for women.
- Involve the private sector in the delivery of public services, with public accountability.

Rural Financial Services

To achieve broad-based economic growth and to reduce vulnerability, countries must ensure that people and enterprises in rural areas have access to financial services. Many developing countries have no formal financial institutions to provide services. Supply-driven agricultural credit has proven unsustainable and unsuccessful, although many countries still use it.

To encourage innovative approaches, donors must support the development of financial products and institutions that fill the special needs of poor rural clients. Meeting those needs will include developing financial instruments for income generation and for reduction of financial risk and recognizing the multiplicity of potential delivery mechanisms, suppliers, and users of rural financial services. To this end, donors will do the following:

- Continue to expand their menu of instruments in rural financing and test them for effectiveness, replicability, and sustainability.
- Continue to support the provision of credit to farm and rural nonfarm enterprises where market failures inhibit the flow of liquidity, while observing sound market development approaches and discipline in financial intermediation.
- Work to narrow gaps in knowledge about the relation between financial services and poverty.

ENHANCED AGRICULTURAL PRODUCTIVITY
AND COMPETITIVENESS

With so many poor rural residents and so many changes in the agricultural sector—compounded by the deteriorating natural resource base—enhancements in agriculture have never been more important for achieving antipoverty goals. International experience has demonstrated the direct relationship between agricultural growth and rural poverty reduction (box 2.1). Agricultural development also induces economic growth in other rural sectors by generating demand for inputs and by providing materials for processing and marketing industries.

Box 2.1   The Agricultural Growth–Poverty Reduction Connection

- A 1 percent increase in agricultural gross domestic product per capita led to a 1.6 percent gain in the per capita incomes of the poorest fifth of the population in 35 countries analyzed (Timmer 1997).
- A 10 percent increase in crop yields led to a reduction of between 6 percent and 10 percent in the number of people living on less than US$1 a day (Irz and others 2001). In Africa, a 10 percent increase in yields resulted in a 9 percent decrease in the same income group.
- In the absence of international agricultural research, wheat prices would have risen 34 percent, and rice prices 41 percent, more between 1970 and 1995.
- The average real income of small farmers in southern India rose by 90 percent, and that of landless laborers rose by 125 percent, in 1973–94 as a result of the "green revolution" (Hazell and Ramasamy 1991).

Refocusing the Agenda for Agriculture

The development community's support for agriculture has important new features, including shifting the emphases to the following:

- From a narrow agricultural focus to a broader policy context—including global effects.
- From agriculture to the entire rural space.
- From crop and livestock yields to market demands and incomes.
- From staples to high-value crops.
- From primary production to the entire food chain.

- From a single-farm approach to heterogeneity.
- From public to public-private partnerships, including community-driven development.
- From avoidance of issues to a head-on approach, especially in biotechnology, forestry, water.

Agriculture is the leading productive sector in the rural economy, closely linked to the nonfarm sector. The production of staple foods is the main source of income for many poor rural households, but to get out of the poverty trap they must diversify into livestock, cash crops, and nonfarm activities. Agricultural investments are more effective if made within appropriate policy and institutional environments with adequate infrastructure and market development (box 2.2).

Providing Sustainable Intensification through the Application of Science

Most high-potential agricultural areas have now reached the limits of land and water resources that can be exploited. The closing of that land—not to mention the acute water scarcity in many areas, diminishing returns, and negative environmental effects from high levels of external inputs—means that future growth in those areas

---

Box 2.2 Underlying Success Factors in Agricultural Development

- Policies must neither discriminate against agriculture nor give it special privileges. Thus, for example, agriculture should be taxed lightly, using the same progressiveness and instruments that are used in other sectors.
- The economy should be open, employment sensitive, and oriented toward smallholders.
- The importance of external markets, including specialty and niche markets, should be fully recognized and exploited.
- Foreign direct investment should be recognized as an integral part of the agricultural development process.
- Land reform is essential where land is very unequally distributed.
- Rapid technological progress is needed, and both the private and public sectors have important roles to play in research, extension, and financing.
- Rural areas need substantial investment in education, in health, and in infrastructure.
- The needs of women—a neglected group of farmers and farm laborers—must be factored into programs.

will largely depend on the substitution of inputs with knowledge. Thus, future agricultural growth in high-potential areas will increasingly be knowledge based. The growth in total factor productivity that accounted for about one-third of past growth will now need to be the major source of growth in the coming decades (box 2.3).

Box 2.3 Agricultural Technology Generation and Dissemination

New models of partnerships between the private and public sectors, through creating competitive and contractual resource allocation schemes, building producer organizations, and providing farmers with a menu of technology options, are showing positive results on the ground:

- In Brazil, Colombia, and Ecuador, national competitive funds have forged new research partnerships involving the national research institutes, universities, farmer organizations, nongovernmental organizations, the private sector, and foreign and international organizations.
- Projects in Burkina Faso, República Bolivariana de Venezuela, and Uganda are building the capacity of rural producer and community organizations and local governments to contract extension services and monitor their implementation, thus resulting in services that are responding to farmer demands, including demands for information on marketing and business management.
- Several projects are incorporating new technologies, such as research in the new field of genomics to more precisely breed target crops in India and multimedia approaches with new information and Web-based approaches to disseminate information in the Russian Federation.

These models can replace the pure public sector delivery model of the past, which had significant problems of efficiency, relevance, and sustainability in many countries.

Investment in science and technology will play a larger role in the future, as agricultural sectors in all regions face increasing land and water scarcity and greater demand for quality assurance in national and global markets. For very poor countries, increasing agricultural productivity remains the main opportunity for growth and poverty reduction. Science, technology, and knowledge-based investments are also important to support market-driven diversification into high-value crops and livestock products, as well as for the development of sustainable production and marketing systems. Investments need to support traditional research areas such as crop and livestock breeding (box 2.4), integrated crop management, crop-livestock systems, postharvest technology, and food safety, as well as to provide new funding for biotechnology research in many countries and regions.

   Institutional reforms that promote demand-driven and financially sustainable national research and extension systems—systems that include public research institutes, universities, the private sector, nongovernmental organizations, and producer organizations—have proven effective. Strategic alliances with foreign and international public and private research institutions, including collaborative research and development activities with Consultative Group on International Agricultural Research centers and other global programs, will be emphasized to promote access to knowledge. Innovative financing arrangements will be explored to develop mechanisms for regional research programs.

   It will be impossible to achieve the level of research investment needed from the public sector alone. Increased private investment in agricultural research is essential. Stimulating that investment will require an economic environment that offers the private sector a reasonable chance of obtaining a return on its investment. Such an environment must include protection of intellectual property rights, input market systems that permit introduction of new varieties and technologies, and other policy reforms conducive to an efficient market system.

Biotechnology. There is an emerging consensus in the scientific community that biotechnology is likely to be a valuable tool in addressing

---

Box 2.4   Meeting the Challenge of the Livestock Revolution

Projections by the International Food Policy Research Institute (Delgado and others 1999) show an almost doubling of demand for animal products over the next two decades. Along with the dramatic expansion of demand in developing countries has come major pressure for change. Traditional production systems frequently cannot compete with intensive industrial production systems, especially for poultry but also increasingly for swine, fish, and cattle. New intensive production systems confront serious issues regarding

- Environmental sustainability, especially relating to waste management.
- Animal health, both to maintain productivity and to avoid international spread of disease.
- Food safety for livestock products.
- Genetic diversity and loss of germplasm of local breeds.
- Animal welfare—a growing concern, at least in industrial countries.
- Employment standards and conditions for employees in processing plants.

production and nutritional constraints and in developing commodities important to poor producers and consumers. Genes are already available that could help food production in the poorest countries if they were transferred into poor people's crops. Those genes improve tolerances to salt, aluminum, and manganese in soils; give plants greater resistance to insects, viruses, bacteria, and fungi; enrich beta carotene to correct vitamin A deficiency; create more nutritious oils, starches, and amino acids; and improve fatty acid profiles and digestibility for animals.

Despite the promise, biotechnology in general and transgenic research in particular have barely begun to be put to work to address the problems of poor people. So far, large commercial plantings of transgenic crops have been restricted to Argentina, Canada, and the United States, with other countries planting less than 2 percent of the world total. One reason is that much of the research supporting this technology is locked into patents held by a small number of multinational corporations that have had little commercial interest in working on crops with limited markets or funding research for the needs of poor producers. Another reason is a range of concerns about health and the environment.

Biotechnology is a supremely controversial topic, and the controversy is often informed more by ideology and philosophical values than by scientific knowledge. There are different schools of thought about the potential environmental and health effects of transgenic technologies, and a responsible technology agenda needs to take these schools of thought into account. Key issues include access to and adaptive capacity for use of proprietary tools and technologies, management of biological assets, assessment of risk, and benefits of food and environmental safety, especially in regard to biodiversity and genetic integrity of local species. Other issues include models of technology transfer, regional harmonization of regulatory frameworks, and development of international public goods. Current international protocols provide guidance on the formulation and implementation of regulations, and discussions continue on international agreements for biosafety, intellectual property rights, and genetic resources.

Environmentally Sustainable Pest Management Systems. Excessive use of chemical pesticides can pose risks to human health and the environment. Integrated pest management systems can reduce reliance on synthetic chemical pesticides. The promotion of integrated pest management includes (a) support to technology generation (such as through the Consultative Group on International Agricultural Research system and through research and development), (b) support to national policy reforms (such as elimination of pesticide subsidies), and (c) inclusion of integrated pest management in extension and farmer education programs. Another approach in some countries has been to support the development of regulatory and economic frameworks that promote integrated pest management (box 2.5).

Box 2.5   Integrated Pest Management in Mali

Mali depends on cotton production as a cash crop for farmers and for export revenues. About 90 percent of the pesticides imported into the country are used on cotton. In the 1990s, because of pesticide resistance and inappropriate use practices, pesticide costs increased steadily while yields remained stable or declined. Evidence of occupational health problems and pesticide residues in food was mounting. On the basis of a comprehensive status report produced by a local research institution and a stakeholder policy workshop, a special integrated pest management initiative was developed.

The initiative cuts across project components and takes a problem-focused view. Policy reform elements include the expansion of existing participatory farmer training for integrated pest management, strengthening of regulatory controls, capacity building for monitoring of environmental and human health impacts, and adjustment of the fiscal and economic incentive framework (elimination of hidden subsidies for cotton and food crop pesticides, plus provision of sustainable funding for regulatory and training activities through the elimination of import duty exemptions for pesticides).

Increasing the Productivity of Water Use in Agriculture

Fresh water is indispensable for agricultural production, yet this resource is under increasing pressure from population increases and competition with other consuming sectors. In a water-constrained environment, it will be a great challenge to meet growing food demands—demands that are expected to double in the next 50 years. Another challenge is that most of the available quality land is already under irrigation. Any further expansion would be in marginal land or at the cost of valuable forest resources. Irrigated agriculture represents 17 percent of the world's cropped area but accounts for 40 percent of total agricultural production.

So future investment will need to focus on improving the productivity of existing cultivated land, meaning "more crop per drop" and "more crop per land area." Making this kind of improvement will require promoting new policies, institutional arrangements, technologies, and management practices that lead to improved water-use efficiency and increased overall agricultural productivity of the land already under irrigation. To improve irrigation efficiency, countries should focus on the following:

- Ensuring the integrity of existing infrastructure that can be economically viable (a challenge in low-income countries and in Central Asia).
- Addressing adverse environmental impacts.
- Providing demand-driven irrigation to improve the livelihoods of poor producers.
- Improving cost-effectiveness.

Future irrigation projects must be designed in concert with agricultural policies. They must include user ownership and incentives for efficient and equitable water use, as well as for cost recovery, and must transfer system responsibilities to autonomous private user groups or water-user associations. Developing countries will require support for innovations to improve water-use efficiency, including, where appropriate, pricing water and shifting from staple food production to higher-value products. The focus on the entire watershed—including attention to downstream environmental effects, accountability and transparency mechanisms, knowledge and information systems, and modernization and rehabilitation—will help realize the potential of existing irrigation systems and reduce the need for new construction. New systems will generally be smaller, and existing larger systems will be renovated in conjunction with management improvements. Attempts will be made to focus management at the greatest level of decentralization possible. If a focus on poverty underpins new investments, irrigation investments can be used to increase the assets of subsistence and small-scale family farmers.

Promoting Diversified and Sustainable Production Systems for Expanding Markets

The food and agricultural systems of today face faster changes than at any time in history. They also face greater opportunities. Those changes and opportunities are being made possible by consumer demands and by the liberalization of markets and trade.

With market liberalization taking hold in most countries, the private sector—traders, processors, and retailers—is expanding in many fields, including technology, information, and marketing services. Markets are now the driver for agricultural growth, making cash crops attractive and allowing specialization and diversification into new products. Private investment is creating more value added and employment in rural space; is generating more competition; and is thus resulting in better services for consumers, farmers, and nonagricultural businesses. Technological progress is central to competitiveness and can boost production for markets and promote specialization and diversification.

National food markets are rapidly changing with urbanization, and more affluent populations are demanding a richer, more diverse diet, with higher-value products. Increases in demand for meat, fruits, vegetables, and specialty and processed foods will provide new market opportunities for farmers, especially those who have access to resources, information, and skills. The dramatic shift in food consumption to urban areas will also place special demands on food supply chains, market infrastructure, and transportation.

Rapidly expanding export markets are providing a new source of rural growth, especially for middle-income countries and the more commercially oriented farmers. Many high-value products—such as fresh fruit, vegetables, fish, and flowers—have created opportunities for developing world farmers to compete for a share in export markets. Diversification to high-value export commodities offers farmers new opportunities to increase incomes without increasing farm area. It also offers them wage employment in processing and packing sites.

Another new phenomenon is that large food retailers and processors are increasingly sourcing their supplies globally. As a result, international trade in high-value agricultural products is growing by some 7 percent annually compared with 2 percent annually for staple commodities. This expanding global market provides exciting possibilities for export, but it also forces farmers to compete with the world's most efficient producers. Conversely, the expansion of supermarkets and chain retail outlets in many developing countries is already having an effect on national production and market systems. In

Latin America and Southeast Asia, for example, local commodities supplied to local markets are having to compete with globally sourced commodities (box 2.6). To achieve gains from diversification requires adequate infrastructure and investment in research and extension.

Growing public awareness of environmental values is leading to new opportunities to produce environmentally friendly products at premium prices. Those opportunities include organic produce, environmental services (such as carbon sequestration or biodiversity conservation), and new products related to multifunctionality of agriculture, including rural landscape management.

Coping with those new market opportunities will require technologies tailored to specific groups of farmers in narrowly defined production environments. Agricultural programs should emphasize technologies that promote more precise use and efficiency of inputs, conservation tillage, and integrated nutrient management. Integrating livestock into small farm systems will provide a means of recycling nutrients and will create opportunities to generate income, especially for women farmers and poor landless people. For both extensive and intensive livestock systems, special attention should go to environmental and food safety issues.

Box 2.6   Malaysia's Export-Oriented Agricultural Growth Based on Cash Crops

Malaysia has achieved success by nurturing its export-oriented cash crops, mainly rubber and oil palm. Malaysia pursued a three-pronged strategy: encouraging rubber production on plantations, developing an oil palm industry on small farms, and increasing rice production in fertile alluvial river basins. The government nurtured the rubber industry by developing rural infrastructure and industry, supporting research that transferred knowledge to farms, and promoting credit and extension programs. It also initiated world-class research in oil palm.

High incomes from oil palm production, export earnings from rubber, and the containment of rice imports provided the resources that kicked off rapid industrialization. Poverty declined, and the Malaysian economy rapidly transformed itself into an industrial one. In Malaysia, political factors contributed to agricultural development because the majority of farmers and government workers were Malays, whereas the majority of businesspeople were Chinese. The only way to avoid income disparities between the two dominant ethnic groups was to create a prosperous agricultural sector.

Strengthening Farmer-to-Market Links

Strengthening farmer-to-market links is crucial in promoting agriculture. Developing countries need to maximize the participation of the private sector and the effect on poverty reduction by the following:

- Improving conditions for private investment and the functioning of markets by helping overcome market failure caused by lack of public goods, market power, and economies of scale; lack of information and skills; and costs of establishing and enforcing agreements.
- Improving the performance of agencies that provide the key public goods and services that underpin the productivity of agriculture, with special focus on cost-effectiveness, client-responsiveness, and sustainability.
- Promoting market solutions for service delivery, including cofinancing and cost recovery mechanisms where they are efficient and effective for poverty reduction.
- Empowering the poor, especially women, through collective action to profitably participate in markets, manage their risks, and access public services.
- Promoting selective direct support to groups of farms, farmers, small enterprises, and rural laborers, with a high potential for sustainable poverty reduction.
- Promoting supply chain management as a means to secure market linkages, control quality, and reduce logistic costs.

Strong producer organizations and community-driven groups are needed to link farmers to markets and technology providers in an enabling environment that is conducive to private investment. Applying information and communication technologies in rural areas may increase the flow of information of all types and facilitate market transactions, changes in employment, emergence of new industries, and social development. New information and communication technologies with lower costs, combined with the increasing literacy and sophistication of farmers, have the potential to revolutionize rural information systems, providing more and better information directly to farmers or to extension agents, agribusinesses, and other intermediaries that serve them.

Fostering Nonfarm Economic Growth

If poverty is to be reduced, a flourishing agricultural sector is essential in most developing countries, but agriculture alone cannot do the whole job. Rural communities also need nonfarm income–producing activities. Those activities, often with linkages to agriculture and natural resources, have important multiplier effects. They are also an important source of employment for rural women.

- *Strengthening skills and organization capital.* For labor-market and enterprise development in rural communities, the skills needed range from functional literacy and numeracy, to specific labor-market skills, to managerial and administrative skills for enterprise development, including market assessments and detection of business opportunities. Close attention should go to women's demands and needs. Why? Because growth in nonfarm activities is linked to declines in poverty, but the declines are faster for woman-headed households.
- *Promoting local economic development and intersectoral linkages.* Cross-ministerial and other working groups levels should address local-level competitiveness and the wider enabling environment of both the farm and nonfarm sectors. They should identify barriers (such as those found in legislation, regulatory frameworks, taxation, infrastructure, financial institutions) and seek means to remove them.
- *Strengthening the supply chain and product linkages.* Trends in consumer markets, quality requirements, and competition require better planning and coordination of supply chains from input suppliers, primary producers, traders, and processors to retailers. Competitiveness depends on effective and flexible logistics and low transaction costs within the chain. The public sector's roles are to create adequate conditions for the development of efficient supply chains in the private sector, to promote investment in physical infrastructure, and to support effective subcontracting systems and quality inspections through appropriate legal frameworks and enforcement systems.
- *Supporting micro, small, and medium-size enterprises.* The development of small rural enterprises requires first and foremost a good investment climate. Especially in rural areas, the development of

small and medium-size enterprises is inhibited by the lack of a skilled labor force and public and private financial, technological, and other services. That is why developing countries need to support commercial business development services (box 2.7) and efficient service delivery, especially with respect to rural infrastructure.

Box 2.7   Kenyan Entrepreneurs Building a Market for Business Services

The Kenya Micro and Small Enterprise Training and Technology Project, an innovative World Bank project with a rural component, has been using vouchers since 1998 to enable small, local rural entrepreneurs to purchase skills and management training. As a demand-side instrument, the voucher project departs from the old approach of supporting public training institutions. Now, diverse suppliers are packaging their services for rural entrepreneurial clients. Skilled craft workers have emerged as the leading providers of training. Local private agencies handle voucher allocation.

More than 25,000 vouchers have been issued to entrepreneurs, 60 percent of them to women. Among training recipients, employment and income have increased 50 percent. The project subsidizes up to 90 percent of the cost of each voucher, but entrepreneurs' cost-sharing percentages rise with second and third vouchers. Rural entrepreneurs now frequently purchase training without vouchers from providers who have demonstrated the value of their services.

Enhancing the Sustainability of Natural Resource Management

Agriculture, as a heavy consumer of natural resources—especially water and soil nutrients—has an obligation to conserve them. Many producers are already concerned about the deteriorating land and water bases in their areas. And public awareness of environmental issues adds urgency to the search for solutions to conservation issues, many of them global. Increasing the efficiency and sustainability of water use in agriculture and improving irrigation system performance are key strategic conservation goals. Ensuring the sustainability of intensive agricultural production systems will require careful management of natural resources, especially in fragile production environments (see chapter 7).

CONCLUSIONS

Given that the world will have to feed an extra 2 billion or 3 billion people over the next 30 to 50 years, achieving responsible growth in rural areas is an urgent need. Recent trends show that rural poverty is persistent and that growth in agricultural production has stagnated. Reversing those trends will require efforts in both the industrial and the developing world. Industrial countries need to liberalize access to their markets and to reduce the agricultural subsidies that distort production. Developing countries need to improve agricultural policies and remove the antirural bias in their development policies. Intensification of land use must be based on new, socially responsible science. Increasing the productivity of water use will benefit agriculture as well as other sectors. Strengthening farmer-to-market links will improve incentives and increase efficiency. Fostering nonfarm growth will increase the dynamism of rural economies. Finally, all of those efforts must be built on efforts to increase the sustainability of natural resource management.

REFERENCES

Delgado, C., M. Rosegrant, H. Steinfeld, S. Ehui, and C. Courbois. 1999. "Livestock to 2020: The Next Food Revolution." Washington, D.C.: International Food Policy Research Institute.

Hazell, P., and C. Ramasamy. 1991. *The Green Revolution Reconsidered: The Impact of High-Yielding Rice Varieties in South India*. Baltimore, Md.: Johns Hopkins Press.

Irz, X., L. Lin, C. Thirtle, and S. Wiggins. 2001. "Agricultural Growth and Poverty Alleviation." *Development Policy Review* 19(4):449–66.

OECD (Organisation for Economic Co-operation and Development). 2002. *Agricultural Policies in OECD Countries*. Paris.

Timmer, C. P. 1997. "How Well Do the Poor Connect to the Growth Process?" Consulting Assistance on Economic Reform Discussion Paper 178. Harvard Institute for International Development, Cambridge, Mass.

World Bank. 2003a. *Reaching the Rural Poor—A renewed strategy for rural development*. Washington, D.C.

_____. 2003b. *Global Economic Prospects and the Developing Countries 2004: Realizing the Development Promise of the Doha Agenda*. Washington, D.C.

CHAPTER 3

TRADE AS AN ENGINE OF RESPONSIBLE GROWTH

The past two decades witnessed a boom in world trade, and although trade expansion slowed with the global recession in 2001–02, the growth in trade has been accelerating, spurring the quickening pace of economic activity around the globe. In this time period, exports from developing countries outpaced those of high-income countries, and their market share rose from roughly 25 percent to 33 percent (figure 3.1).

Moreover, developing countries' share of manufacturing rose sharply. In the 1990s alone, the share of developing countries in global trade rose by more than 7 percentage points. For all regions, manufactures rose from less than 30 percent of export earnings on average to more than 70 percent. Almost all regions increased the technological content of their exports (see figure 3.1).

These increases reflect the growing competitiveness of exports of developing countries in global markets (figure 3.2). Although only the East Asia and Pacific region benefited from above-average growth in demand for their products, exports of all regions except the Middle East and North Africa grew faster than the world average thanks to greater competitiveness. In the 1990s, for example, South Asia's exports grew 45 percent faster than the global average. About two-thirds of this growth was associated with increases in market

This chapter was written by Bernard Hoekman, Denis Medvedev, and Richard Newfarmer of the Development Prospects Group and Development Research Group.

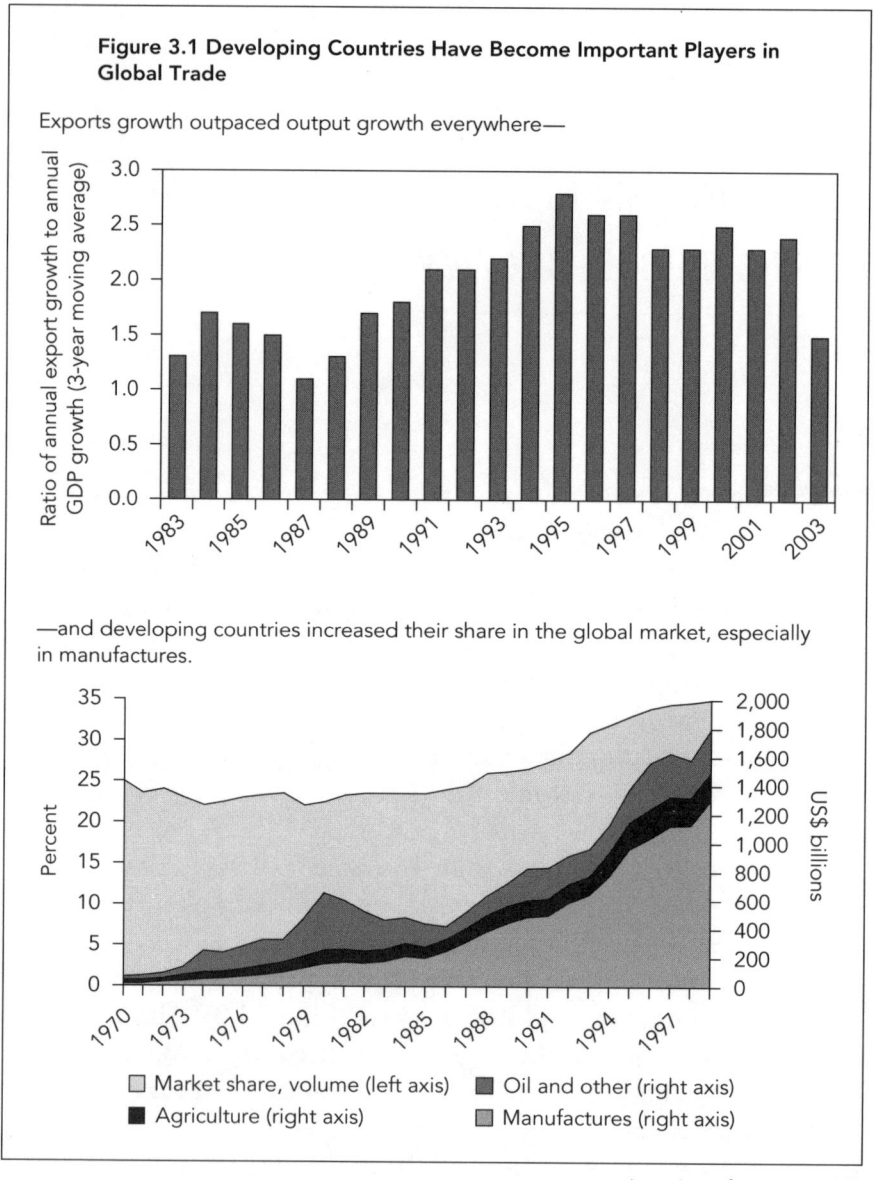

Figure 3.1 Developing Countries Have Become Important Players in Global Trade

Exports growth outpaced output growth everywhere—

—and developing countries increased their share in the global market, especially in manufactures.

(continued on page 43)

share (competitiveness) and one-third with increases in the growth of export markets (demand).

However, not all the news was good. The poorest countries generally did less well than their middle-income counterparts, partly because of the dependence of their foreign exchange earnings on agricultural commodities and labor-intensive manufactures. Several

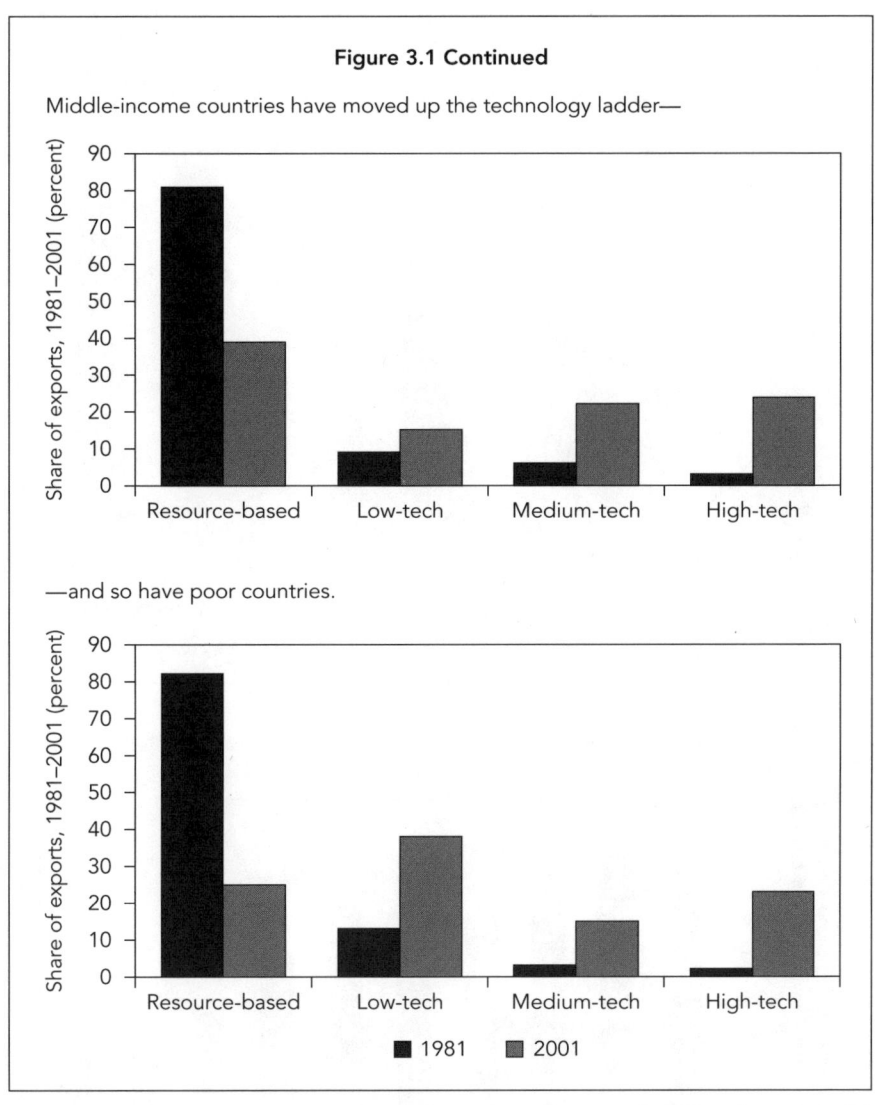

Figure 3.1 Continued

Middle-income countries have moved up the technology ladder—

—and so have poor countries.

(continued on page 44)

reasons explain this poor performance in the case of agriculture: high protection in major markets limits trade, improvements in technology have benefited middle- and high-income countries more than the poorest countries, and expanding supply has produced a downward global price trend. All these factors are complicated by low income elasticities of demand for food.

Often, however, problems on the supply side of the market were even more fundamental. Civil conflicts undermined all economic

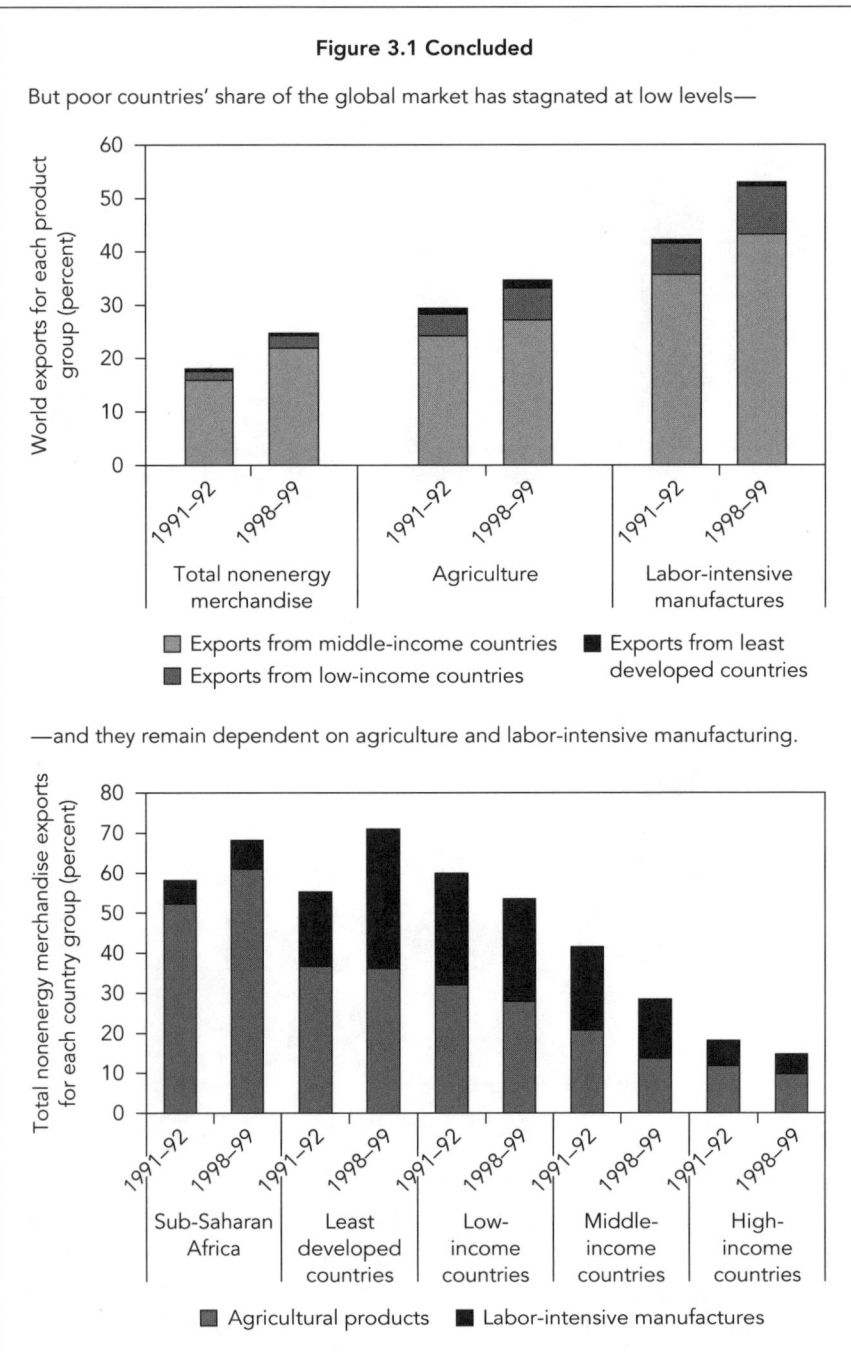

Figure 3.1 Concluded

But poor countries' share of the global market has stagnated at low levels—

■ Exports from middle-income countries   ■ Exports from least
■ Exports from low-income countries   developed countries

—and they remain dependent on agriculture and labor-intensive manufacturing.

■ Agricultural products   ■ Labor-intensive manufactures

Source: World Bank data.

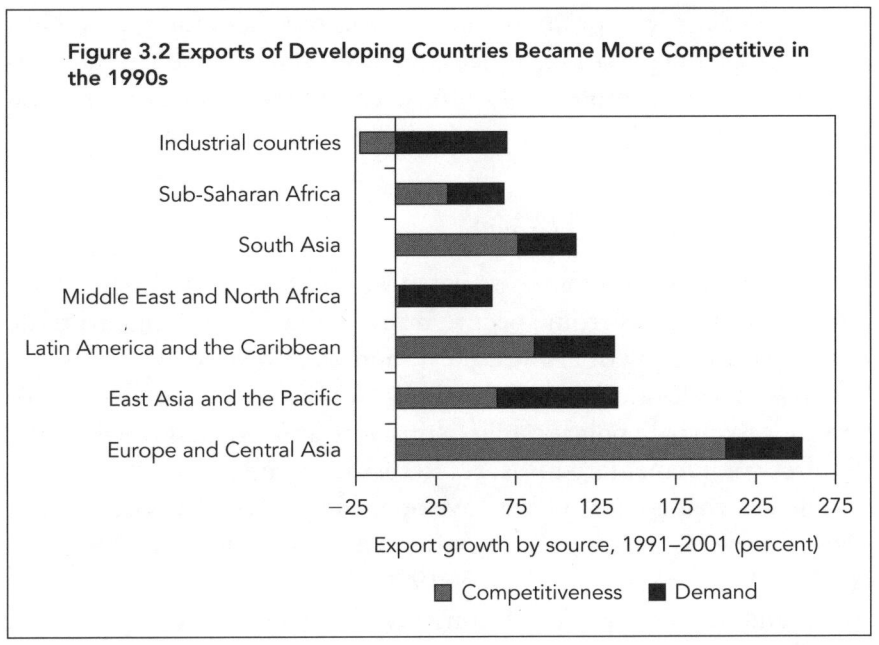

Figure 3.2 Exports of Developing Countries Became More Competitive in the 1990s

Export growth by source, 1991–2001 (percent)

■ Competitiveness ■ Demand

Source: World Bank 2003.

performance in a score of African countries, and poor macroeconomic policies led to huge price disadvantages as a result of overvalued currencies. Moreover, governance problems, corruption, and institutional weaknesses worsened the local investment climate and inhibited local entrepreneurs from taking advantage of market opportunities. Those same factors induced instability in commodity prices and had adverse impacts on the demand for commodity exports.

TRADE, GROWTH, AND POVERTY REDUCTION

Trade can be a powerful engine of sustainable economic growth and poverty reduction. But the relationship between trade and growth is complex and is not automatic. A trade minister cannot simply pull the lever labeled "improved trade policy" and expect that trade will boom, economic growth will accelerate, and the poor will benefit. Instead, governments everywhere have to pursue a mix of policies to get the trade engine running smoothly. The international community—rich and poor countries working together—can use the trade agreements, and the Doha negotiations in particular, to improve their trade policies, support the implementation of complementary policies, and create new opportunities for developing countries.

Trade Is Associated with Growth

Greater trade integration is associated with faster growth (figure 3.3).[1] That said, the links from specific trade policy instruments to trade outcomes and growth are less clear, and controversy over causality abounds. The lesson from the analyses swirling around these controversies is that trade policy can help promote and sustain growth, but it requires complementary measures to realize its full potential.

The fact that countries that have opened up to trade have also been able to grow faster has been documented extensively in the literature (Dollar 1992; Frankel and Romer 1999; Rodriguez and Rodrik 1999; Sachs and Warner 1995). Although problems in these studies have been highlighted, the issues identified by critics question the exact nature of the relationship more than its existence: "Even though no one study can establish that openness to trade has unambiguously helped the representative Third World economy, the preponderance of evidence supports this conclusion" (Lindert and Williamson 2001).

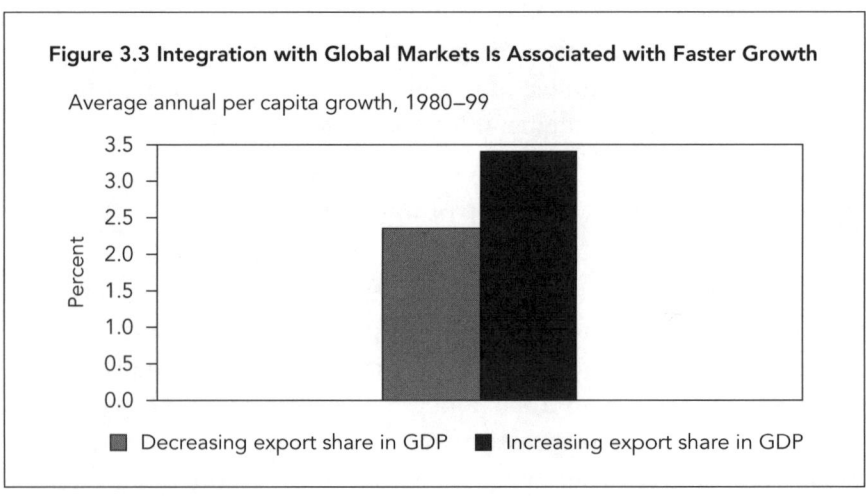

Figure 3.3 Integration with Global Markets Is Associated with Faster Growth

Average annual per capita growth, 1980–99

■ Decreasing export share in GDP   ■ Increasing export share in GDP

Source: World Bank 2001.

Dollar and Kraay (2001) charted the association between trade and growth by looking at a sample of 72 developing countries that they divided into two groups: the "globalizers"—the 24 countries that saw the greatest increase in their ratios of trade to gross domestic product (GDP) between 1975–79 and 1995–97—and the "nonglobalizers." The globalizers grew faster and outpaced both the nonglobalizers and the industrial countries over the past two decades (figure 3.4).

This line of research has been criticized on the grounds that measures of trade policy are inadequate, trade reforms are often inextricably linked to other reforms and institutional improvements, and trade outcomes are endogenous to growth itself.[2] More recent research seeks to overcome some of these difficulties through microeconomic analysis of trade-induced changes at the industry or firm level. These studies can shed light on trade being the mechanism of growth (Hallak and Levinsohn 2004). For example, opening a country to trade opportunities will typically increase the variety of imports available and may also increase the variety of exports, both of which contribute to productivity growth and, hence, aggregate growth.

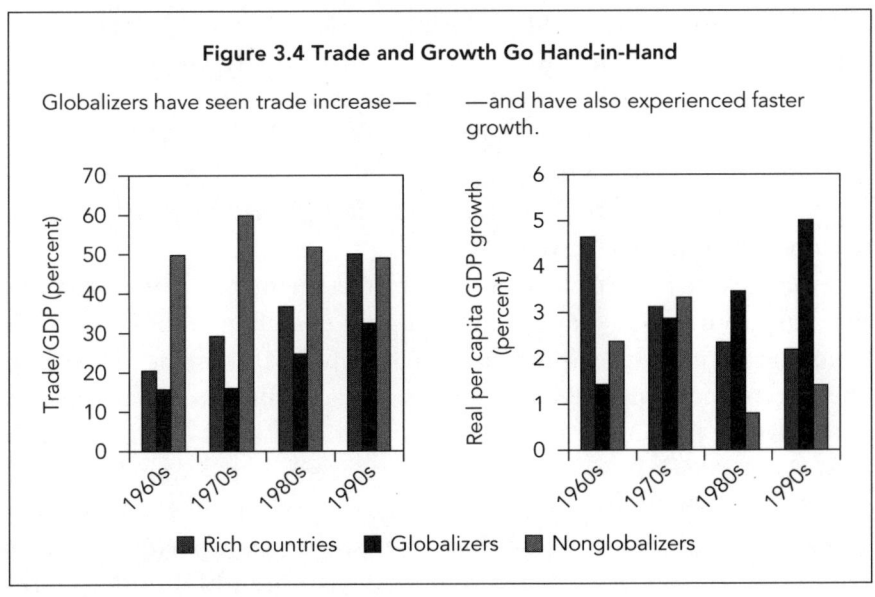

Figure 3.4 Trade and Growth Go Hand-in-Hand

Globalizers have seen trade increase— —and have also experienced faster growth.

Source: Dollar and Kraay 2001.

For a sample of 34 countries from 1982 to 1997, more than 50 percent of country productivity differences can be explained by the differences in industry export variety.[3] The implication for policy is that in trade, trade integration through increases in product variety is an important channel that leads to aggregate growth. The product variety of the exporting countries depends on the trade policies of the importing countries and the distance between the trading partners (Feenstra and Kee 2004b). These findings suggest that lowering trade barriers in importing countries may mean that exporting countries may enjoy a productivity boost, attributable to a greater variety in their exports. The implication for policy is that trade integration (openness) is an important determinant of growth. Other studies have shown that import competition can raise domestic productivity (Muendler 2004).

Significant attention has been devoted to the role of trade in transferring knowledge across international borders, because diffusion of knowledge is one of the basic factors underpinning growth. Several studies have examined the effect of research and development (R&D), as embodied in trade, on total factor productivity in developing countries (Schiff and Wang 2003; Schiff, Olarreaga, and Wang 2002). Moreover, trade-related R&D spillovers may occur in interaction with other policies. High levels of education and better governance increase productivity levels not only directly but also through their interaction with foreign R&D as embodied in trade in R&D-intensive industries (Schiff and Wang 2004). These results imply the existence of potential virtuous growth cycles and suggest that simultaneous reforms of trade, education, and governance may have a greater effect on productivity.

Greater openness to foreign direct investment (FDI) may serve as another channel for facilitating technology diffusion and thus economic growth in developing countries. Bank research has focused on the effects operating across industries, because multinationals have an incentive to prevent knowledge dissipation to local competitors in host economies but may benefit from transferring technology to local suppliers. Recent empirical analysis at the firm level for Lithuania found evidence consistent with such positive productivity spillovers from FDI: an increase of one standard deviation in FDI in the sourcing sectors was associated with an increase of 15 percent in output for each domestic firm in the supplying industry (Javorcik Smarzynska forthcoming). Related work finds that interindustry spillovers may be greater in projects with shared domestic and foreign ownership than for fully owned foreign investments.[4]

Similarly, although trade liberalization may be necessary, it is not a sufficient condition to promote growth. Trade does little to stimulate growth in economies with excessive regulation. Cross-country analysis shows that increased openness to trade is positively correlated with income in all countries, as expected (see figure 3.4) but, if anything, is associated with a lower standard of living in heavily regulated economies (figure 3.5).[5] Excessive regulations reduce incomes because resources are prevented from moving to the most productive sectors and firms following liberalization. When the effect of trade on growth in more regulated economies is controlled for, the evidence that trade positively affects growth is stronger.

Trade's Relation to Poverty Is Indirect

Trade is thus an opportunity, not a guarantee. If trade reforms are to promote growth through improved price incentives, other policies

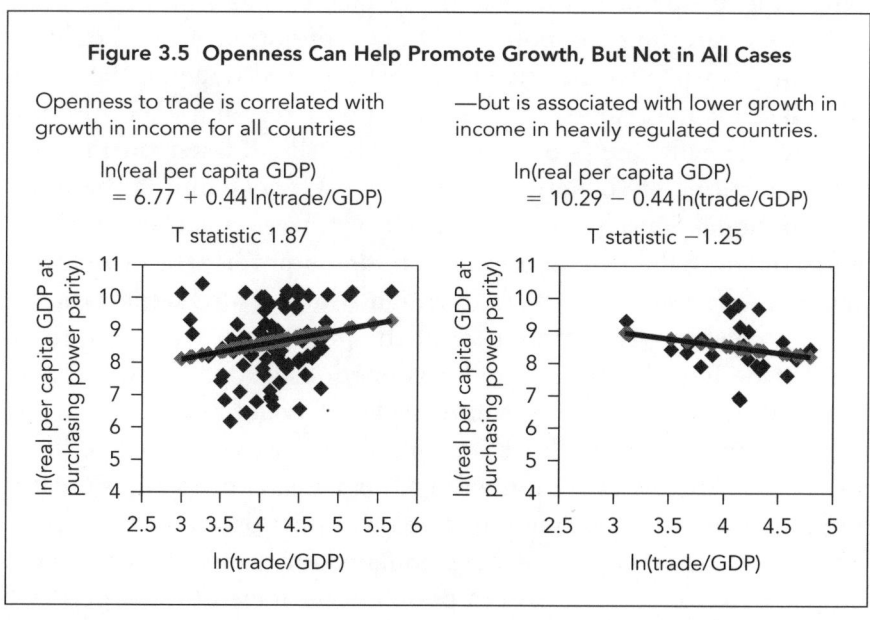

Figure 3.5 Openness Can Help Promote Growth, But Not in All Cases

Openness to trade is correlated with growth in income for all countries

—but is associated with lower growth in income in heavily regulated countries.

ln(real per capita GDP)
= 6.77 + 0.44 ln(trade/GDP)

T statistic 1.87

ln(real per capita GDP)
= 10.29 − 0.44 ln(trade/GDP)

T statistic −1.25

Source: Bolaky and Freund 2004.

are needed to ensure that investment flows into internationally competitive sectors and that weak or corrupt institutions do not undercut the positive incentives. Competition policy that is broadly defined to include the labor market and the regulation of entry is particularly important: firms (and factors of production) must be able to enter new areas and to exit declining, unprofitable activities. As discussed below, policies affecting the performance of service sectors are also critical—the availability, quality, and cost of services are a key determinant of the competitiveness of firms in a market (and the attractiveness of a given location for investment).

Even when trade raises average incomes, its effects on poverty will depend on whether poverty in a given country is sensitive to growth in average incomes and on how the increase in trade affects the distribution of income in the country. The effect of income growth is empirically well understood. The sensitivity of poverty to growth in average incomes depends in an important way on initial inequalities in a country (Ravallion 1997). When incomes and opportunities are distributed fairly equally, the effect of growth on poverty is larger than when initial inequality is high. So the growth associated with increased trade (or from any other source) is likely to have larger proportional effects on poverty in countries where initial inequality is low.

More interesting and potentially more important from a political economy perspective are the effects of increased trade on the distribution of income. Almost by definition, if increased trade disproportionately benefits the poor, poverty levels will fall faster than if trade disproportionately benefits the nonpoor. Understanding the likely distributional consequences of trade liberalization is thus crucial to understanding the overall effects of trade on poverty. In many cases, there are very direct channels through which trade liberalization is likely to disproportionately benefit the poor. For example, agricultural trade liberalization that allows previously suppressed prices of agricultural goods to rise to world levels will benefit farmers, who are net producers, but will hurt consumers. If farmers are more likely to be poor, the liberalization will be, on average, propoor. Similarly, reductions in tariffs on manufactures will hurt previously protected urban workers, who in many developing countries are likely to be relatively well off, but will benefit poorer consumers of these products by lowering prices.

At the same time, however, the distributional consequences of trade liberalization can also work against poor people. For example, reductions in tariffs imply reductions in trade tax revenues, which can be important in developing countries that rely disproportionately on this source of revenue. To the extent that public spending disproportionately benefits poor people (and this is by no means universal), reductions in tax revenues that accompany trade liberalization can have adverse distributional consequences by affecting transfers from the government.

The distributional consequences of trade liberalization are, therefore, complex and country specific. Determining whether a given action would be propoor or antipoor requires careful analysis, some of which is discussed below. Looking back across countries, one finds little evidence that increased trade is systematically associated with either increases or decreases in inequality (figure 3.6).

Trade can have a disproportionately positive effect on incomes of the poor because it has the potential to raise returns to the factor in

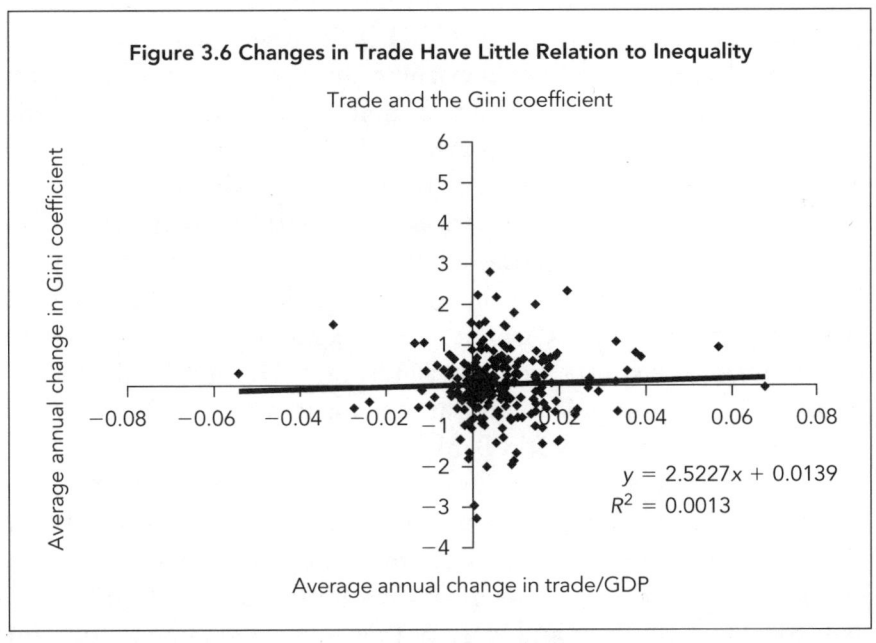

Figure 3.6 Changes in Trade Have Little Relation to Inequality

Trade and the Gini coefficient

$y = 2.5227x + 0.0139$
$R^2 = 0.0013$

Average annual change in Gini coefficient

Average annual change in trade/GDP

Note: This figure shows changes in trade as a fraction of GDP and changes in the Gini measure of income inequality for a large sample of growth episodes of at least 5 years in duration.
Source: Dollar and Kraay 2001.

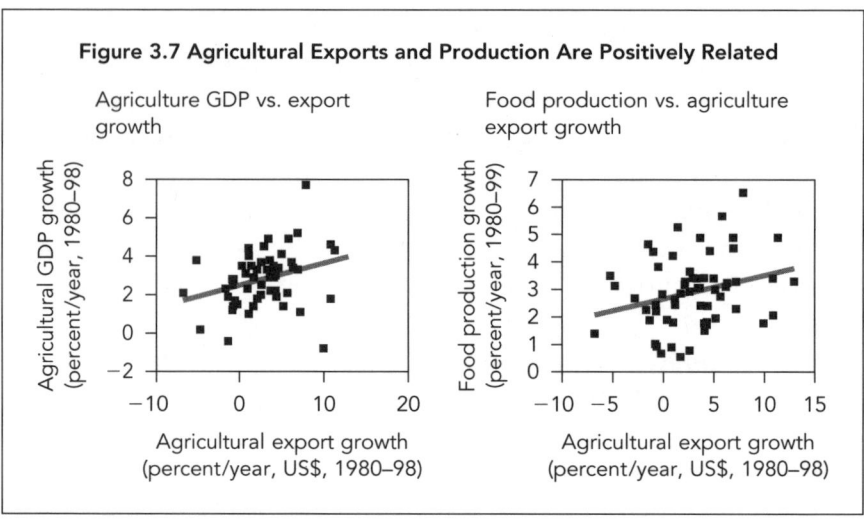

Figure 3.7 Agricultural Exports and Production Are Positively Related

Source: World Bank 2001.

which the poor are abundant—labor.[6] Agriculture and labor-intensive manufactures are especially important to the poor. In agriculture, greater export growth has been linked to higher agricultural GDP and more food production (figure 3.7). Thus, trade in agriculture has been found to raise rural incomes and reduce poverty. It is important to note that greater exports did not come at the expense of domestic production, which would have severely curbed any development impact of increased trade. Instead, the relationship between trade and production is positive, because foreign exchange earnings from food exports can be used to purchase additional inputs and, therefore, raise agricultural growth. Individual country studies support the results of cross-country estimates: Uganda, Vietnam, and other countries were able to increase exports, boost agricultural GDP and food production, and significantly decrease rural poverty in the 1990s following liberalization reforms (World Bank 2001).

In addition to combating rural poverty through growth in agriculture, trade can reduce urban poverty by expanding markets for labor-intensive manufactures. Because of their low labor costs, most developing countries have a comparative advantage in industries such as textiles and clothing and can use this advantage as an engine for growth and development. Over the 1990s, developing countries expanded their share of global trade in textiles and clothing. Since

1981, the average annual growth rate of exports of textiles from low-income countries was 14 percent, compared with a growth rate of 5 percent in high-income countries (World Bank 2003). Case studies from Bangladesh, Pakistan, and Tunisia show that these countries were able to reduce poverty significantly as their textile and clothing exports boomed (World Bank 2001). Since the majority of textiles and clothing manufacturing is concentrated in urban areas, the reduction in urban poverty was even more pronounced—urban poverty head-count was reduced by 30 percent in Bangladesh and more than 25 percent in Tunisia. In Mauritius, the growth of the textile and clothing sector increased wages by nearly 50 percent (World Bank 2001).

Understanding the effects of trade liberalization on poverty is important in designing trade reforms to ensure that the reforms will help achieve poverty reduction goals. Aside from the obvious moral imperative, reducing poverty is important to facilitate the building of broad ownership of reforms, thereby making them more sustainable. Because the effects of trade (and trade reforms) on poverty depend on a large number of factors that vary across countries, research on this subject has been microeconometric and simulation based.[7] The methodology has been developed in the past few years and is based on two links: one connecting trade policies to prices of a disaggregated bundle of goods and another connecting those prices to household welfare.[8]

Trade barriers generally raise domestic prices of traded goods above world prices, thus affecting households insofar as they consume or derive income from the affected goods (either directly or through employment, that is, wages). Ex post analyses of trade liberalization undertaken for Argentina, Ethiopia, and Mexico, among others, suggest that the poor generally benefit from liberalization, but that liberalization can also increase income inequality, as in the case of Ethiopia and Mexico (see Ianchovichina, Nicita, and Soloaga 2001; Nicita and Olarreaga 2003; Porto 2003a). The reason is that protection tends to be higher on relatively skill-intensive goods; thus, tariff removal has tended to benefit the poor over those better off. In Ethiopia, existing tariffs protect the richest households two times more than the poorest. Not all households gain. Those that have little access to credit or that are located in remote areas where self-subsistence farming is prevalent may not gain or may gain much less.

In Mexico, for example, northern states have seen much more reduction in poverty than southern ones. Analysis of the potential effect of complete trade liberalization in Ethiopia suggests that, on average, real incomes of the poor would increase by 5 percent but that some 12 percent of the poor could suffer a decline in income. This analysis illustrates the need for complementary policies and safety nets.[9] Research on Argentina concludes that trade liberalization (free trade) would lower the number of people living in poverty by 0.6 to 1.7 percentage points. Moreover, liberalization by trading partners would reduce the number by 1.4 to 2.9 percentage points for a total of 1.7 to 4.6 points, or between 7 percent and 18 percent of the baseline (Porto 2003b).

In sum, generalizations about the trade-poverty link are elusive. Although the poor generally are found to benefit from trade reforms, the effects in any given country depend on the pass-through of price changes, wage-price elasticities, and factor intensities. Even if the poor gain on average, selected individuals or regions may lose. Aggregate results mask substantial variation in poverty changes by individual household groups and by type of policy. For example, some studies have found that skilled labor may fare better than unskilled labor, which can be attributed to relatively higher initial tariffs on unskilled labor–intensive products. Such variation underscores the important role of government in providing support for adversely affected groups as trade expands.

DEVELOPMENT AND THE PROMISE OF THE DOHA DEVELOPMENT AGENDA

The global trading system, which is rife with barriers that prevent the products of the world's poor from reaching markets, has yet to reach its development potential. Although the Uruguay Round successfully lowered barriers in manufacturing, including the removal of quantitative restrictions on exports of textiles and clothing, and for the first time extended multilateral disciplines to agriculture, much remains to be done to make the world trading system more propoor. The new disciplines in agriculture proved largely ineffective at providing market access. In fact, in the years after the conclusion of the Uruguay

Round, developing countries' share of agricultural markets in the industrial countries actually fell. In other sectors, tariff peaks and tariff escalation in key products, as well as the imposition of specific duties and antidumping measures, hinder the ability of low-income countries to move up the development ladder.

Improving labor standards is a fundamental aspect of responsible growth. However many developing nations have resisted efforts to include labor standards in world trade agreements. Proponents argue that trade sanctions should be used to enforce labor standards and to raise wages, whereas developing countries fear that international labor standards could become masks for protection. The inclusion of developing countries in the World Trade Organization (WTO) threatens a main comparative advantage of developing countries (box 3.1). Environmental standards, another fundamental aspect of responsible

---

Box 3.1 Improving Labor Standards

Numerous studies have shown that low labor standards that affect working conditions do not grant a competitive edge to developing countries. According to a 1996 study by the Organisation for Economic Co-operation and Development, countries with lower core labor standards (core labor standards include proscriptions on exploitative child labor, on forced labor, on discrimination in employment, and on failure to recognize freedom of association and the right to collective bargaining) do not have an improved export performance (OECD 1996). The study finds no correlation between real wage growth and the degree of respect for freedom of association. However, it supports the view that higher national income levels and open-market reforms are both associated with improved labor standards.

At the same time, trade sanctions to improve labor conditions are likely to be counterproductive. By limiting trade between nations, sanctions shackle the growth in wages that expanded trade would otherwise bring. Historically, the growth rate of wages has been twice as rapid in developing countries that increased their trade participation in the world economy as compared with those that did not (Collier and Dollar forthcoming). Moreover, their wage growth has been even faster than in the rich countries. Depriving poor nations of export opportunities in the name of raising wages is fatuous.

There are other problems with trade sanctions. Trade sanctions penalize whole countries and industries when the violators are firms—and often they are firms that do not export. Firms serving the domestic market usually have worse labor standards than export industries (Aggarwal 1995). Wages and working conditions in export processing zones, for example, tend to be higher than the average for the domestic economy. Trade sanctions would, in effect, target

---

(continued on page 56)

Box 3.1   Continued

the better-performing export firms. Also, trade sanctions are an inherently un-equal instrument: they are likely to be imposed only by industrial countries against developing countries. Finally, trade sanctions can hurt the very people they are intended to help. For example, in Bangladesh, children displaced from garment factories because of the owners' fear of sanctions found alternative em-ployment in activities with even lower standards, such as street vending and prostitution (Pananagariya 1999).

Fortunately, the international community has more effective instruments to promote better labor standards. A main purpose of the International Labour Organization is to promulgate good labor practices and legislations, and it, rather than the WTO, is far better positioned to lead international efforts. Gov-ernments should be encouraged to monitor and enforce their own legislation by, if necessary, imposing fines on enterprises that violate core labor standards (Elliot 2001). Revenues from the fines could be channeled back into enforce-ment programs and investments to upgrade labor conditions.

Such instruments have several advantages over trade sanctions: violators are punished rather than all firms, revenues stay in the country and are used to im-prove standards rather than imposing income losses on countries, and improve-ments occur in a manner consistent with indigenous social values and mores rather than according to the dictates of people in rich countries. If violations are pervasive and egregious and if international sanctions are needed, withholding development assistance can be a more effective instrument (Torres 1996). The role of nongovernmental organizations (NGOs) is important, too. The aggres-sive campaigns of NGOs have called attention to firm violations around the world, and these campaigns can help promulgate stricter codes of conduct, encourage enforcement, and call public and international attention to the most egregious violations (Gereffi, Garcia-Johnson, and Sasser 2001). This suggests that the international community can help developing countries improve wages and working conditions, but can do so better through the International Labour Organization than through the WTO.

Source: World Bank 2001.

growth, are also at the forefront of the public debate on trade. The WTO's Technical Barriers to Trade Agreement and its Agreement on Sanitary and Phytosanitary Standards both include some references to environmental protection and trade, although to date few formal dis-putes have been brought before the WTO (box 3.2).

In November 2001, WTO members launched the Doha Develop-ment Agenda, a new round of global trade talks that aims to harness the reciprocal bargaining process to lower trade barriers of special importance to developing countries. The agenda includes market access in agriculture, tariff reductions in manufactured goods, and

Box 3.2   Trade and Environment

The links between trade and the environment are complex. One effect is that trade can raise scales of production. This effect will be negative because the amount of resources used and the amount of pollution emitted will rise with the level of output. However, if trade induces a change in output composition, it is possible that dirty industries (even at larger scales) may decrease and clean industries may expand, thus counteracting the effects of scale. Trade may also permit greater access to more advanced and cleaner technology. The net effect depends on the change in output mix and technology that occurs with trade-induced growth.

What are the trade consequences of environmental regulation? One hypothesis is that pollution-intensive industries take flight to countries that have lax environmental standards. However, there is limited evidence to date to support this hypothesis (see, for example, Leonard 1988; Pearson 1987).

A second analytical approach considers the environment as a factor of production, like capital and labor. The idea is that countries that have lax environmental regulations (for example, because of an abundance of resources) tend to specialize in pollution-intensive goods. Here, too, the evidence is ambiguous. A study looking at five pollution-intensive industries in 23 countries found that environmental regulations have caused trade patterns to deviate from the predictions of the model (Tobey 1990). And a study of 24 countries with five different pollution-intensive industries found that stringent environmental regulation reduces net exports of the five pollution-intensive industries (Wilson, Sewadeh, and Otsuki 2001). But an investigation of the environmental effects of the North American Free Trade Agreement concluded that lax environmental regulations do not create a comparative advantage in Mexico (Grossman and Krueger 1993). Yet another study using a gravity model to investigate whether differences in environmental regulations have affected bilateral trade in pollution-intensive goods between a sample of industrial and developing countries found no evidence that countries that have stricter environmental standards lower their total exports of pollution-intensive goods (Xu 1999). In sum, the evidence on the specific linkages between environmental regulation and trade is mixed.

So what policy tools and institutions are best suited to promoting higher levels of environmental protection? Trade sanctions to support environmental protection can restrict the market access of developing countries. Indeed, such sanctions may be counterproductive: because environmental regulations tend to improve as incomes rise, policies that restrict trade and restrict growth also undermine a driver of environmental improvement. Also, sanctions penalize whole industries—the clean firms as well as the polluters. Moreover, many polluters produce for the local market and are unaffected by sanctions. Finally, domestic pollution and environmental protection can be controlled most effectively when they are targeted at the source—through taxes and other domestic policy instruments. A more productive approach is to establish policy coordination among countries. Such coordination would allow for joint regulation of common watershed and air basin controls in areas of transborder pollution and

(continued on page 58)

Box 3.2   Continued

for development assistance to transfer clean technology and environmental aid
that would strengthen environmental protection over time. Global environmental agreements (such as the Montreal Protocol, which bans certain ozone-
depleting chemicals) and others, if based on sound cost-benefit analysis, can
raise environmental quality over time. Voluntary eco-labeling programs also
can provide incentives for environmental protection.

Recent analyses focusing on developing countries find little evidence of the
"pollution haven hypothesis" (Eskeland and Harrison 2003). But the empirical
results on U.S. regional data lead to mixed conclusions. One study finds no evidence that this difference has systematically affected the location choices of
manufacturing plants (Levinson 1996). Others show, however, that the annual
designation of air-quality attainment status, which triggers specific equipment
requirements at the county level in the United States, reduces the number of
firms setting up establishments in polluting industries in nonattainment areas
(Becker and Henderson 2000; Keller and Levinson 2002).

Source: World Bank 2001.

liberalization of trade in services. The so-called Singapore issues
were also placed on the agenda, with the objective of launching negotiations related to regulatory requirements in the areas of investment, competition, government procurement, and trade facilitation.
Although developing countries have an interest in each area, they
negotiated to drop everything but trade facilitation from the multilateral discussions because of uncertainty of the benefits of Singapore
issues' inclusion in the WTO negotiating agenda (see Hoekman and
Newfarmer 2003; Newfarmer 2003).

Agriculture Is at the Heart of a Development Round

Agriculture is central to realizing the development promise of this
trade round for two reasons: it is where most of the world's poor
work, and it is where most of the world's protection is. Some 70 percent of the world's poor people live in rural areas and earn their
income from agriculture. Largely exempt from pre–Uruguay Round
trade agreements to reduce protection, agriculture is among the
most distorted sectors in international trade. Even though levels of
average tariff protection are comparable in rich and poor countries,
the extensive use of producer subsidies in the member countries of
the Organisation for Economic Co-operation and Development

(OECD) and the fact that the OECD countries generate two-thirds of world agricultural trade underscore the centrality of OECD policies to development outcomes. Of the gains to be realized from full global liberalization of merchandise trade, reducing protection in agriculture alone would produce roughly two-thirds.

A few facts are enough to establish the context. Protection facing agricultural exporters in developing countries is four to seven times higher than that facing exporters of manufactures in the developed countries and two to three times higher than protection faced by developing countries' exporters of manufactures (International Monetary Fund and World Bank 2002). Tariff peaks against products from poor countries are particularly high in rich countries. Tariff escalation that discourages development of further processing is more pronounced in agriculture in both rich and poor countries (figure 3.8). Hefty specific duties are particularly common in rich countries; these duties automatically increase protection when commodity prices fall, thereby throwing the burden of adjustment onto global prices and poor countries.

Total support to agriculture in OECD countries in the late 1990s amounted to US$330 billion—of which some US$250 billion went directly to producers. Roughly one-third of this support is through budget transfers (subsidies), and two-thirds comes from measures

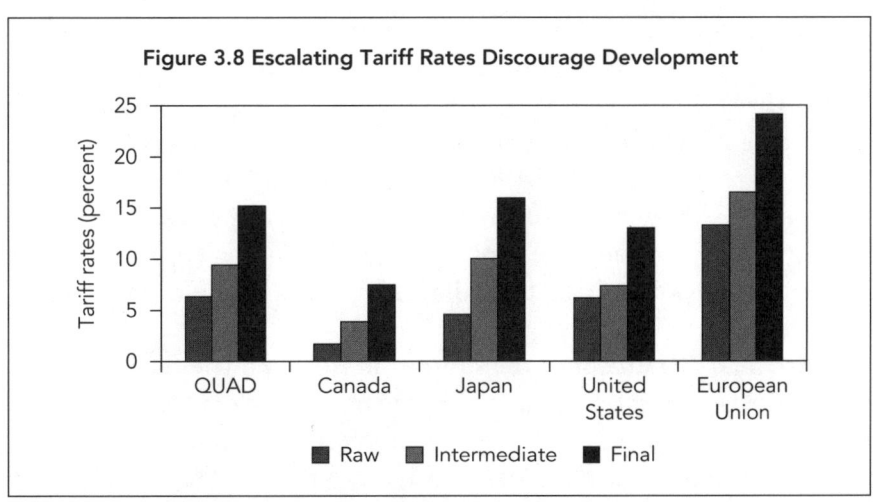

Figure 3.8 Escalating Tariff Rates Discourage Development

Note: QUAD is the average of Canada, Japan, the United States, and the European Union.
Source: World Bank staff.

that raise domestic prices above world levels. Border barriers (tariffs, quotas) are the major instruments through which such support is given and should, therefore, be the priority from a development perspective. The overall effect of this support is to stimulate overproduction in high-cost rich countries and to shut out potentially more competitive products from poor countries. It is no wonder that agricultural exports from developing countries to rich countries grew in the 1990s at just half the rate of agricultural exports to other developing countries.

Consider how agricultural protection plays through individual commodity markets. Sugar in the European Union, Japan, and the United States is commonly protected through a combination of quotas, tariffs, and subsidies that allow domestic sugar producers in those countries to receive more than double the world market price. OECD governments support sugar producers with the equivalent of US$6.4 billion annually—an amount nearly equal to all exports from developing countries. Prices are so high that it has become economical to grow sugar beets in cold climates and to convert corn to high-fructose corn syrup, and sugar imports in the OECD have shrunk to next to nothing.

U.S. subsidies to cotton growers totaled US$3.7 billion in 2002—three times as much as U.S. foreign aid to Africa. These subsidies depress world cotton prices by an estimated 10 to 20 percent, reducing the income of thousands of poor farmers in West Africa and in Central and South Asia—and in poor countries around the world. In West Africa alone, where cotton is a critical cash crop for many small-scale near-subsistence farmers, annual income losses for cotton growers are about US$250 million a year. Rice support in Japan amounts to 700 percent of production at world prices, thus stimulating inefficient domestic production, reducing demand, and denying export opportunities to India, Thailand, Vietnam, and other countries.

More than 70 percent of the support in rich countries is directed to large (often corporate) farmers. These farmers have incomes that are higher—often substantially so—than average incomes in Europe, Japan, and—to a lesser extent—the United States. The net effect of subsidizing the relatively rich in industrial countries at the expense of price penalties for the products of the relatively poor in developing countries is to aggravate global income inequalities. Said differently, subsidies make the rich even richer and the poor even poorer.

Realizing the development potential of Doha requires phased reductions of border protection and subsidies. Of the two, border protection is the most important. In the case of subsidies (budget transfers), what matters is not so much to reduce the outlays but to decouple them from production—that is, to cease making the subsidy a function of (past) output produced. Income transfers are much less trade distorting. Reductions in border protection ought to be done in a way that cuts antidevelopment tariff peaks significantly, reduces tariff escalation, and phases out specific duties. A propoor reform also requires reforming policies that distort particular commodities of importance to developing countries—sugar, cotton, rice, wheat, and dairy products.

Because global prices may rise in some commodities as a result of agricultural liberalization, the international community may want to design—and help finance—a program of adjustment in vulnerable countries that suffer deterioration in their terms of trade. Those effects are likely to be confined, for several reasons, to a few countries. Many food importers also export other agricultural products that will experience positive terms-of-trade changes from liberalization. Other countries now have tariffs on those same food imports, and those tariffs can be reduced to offset any increase in global prices. Some food importers will gain access to new markets in nonagricultural products and be able to export. And because prices will change relatively slowly, some food importers will increase domestic production in response to higher prices and will become self-sufficient or even net exporters. Nonetheless, even though the changes are likely to be manageable at the global level, the issue requires study—and in some countries it may require action.

Because rich and poor countries will both benefit from liberalization, all must make the policy changes necessary to realize its promise. The rich countries, whose policies arguably distort international trade the most, cannot escape leadership on this issue. Leadership among donors to finance a program to cushion adjustment is essential. Moreover, their technical assistance to help implement standards and facilitate trade is needed to help developing countries take advantage of new trade opportunities.

Middle-income countries, whose policy reforms would produce a large share of the benefit to developing countries from global liberalization in agriculture, have to move more assertively than in the past. Their high tariffs have an adverse impact on growing South-South trade, especially with neighboring countries. In a pattern common to all regions, agricultural exporters in East Asia paid one-third of all tariff duties remitted to foreign governments to enter other East Asian markets (second only to tariffs paid to get into rich countries). Agricultural exporters in the Middle East paid 44 percent of their tariff duties to regional neighbors.

Nonfarm Trade Is Essential to Growth in Poor Countries

Over the past two decades, developing countries have increased their share of global trade from just under one-quarter to about one-third. As a group, they have moved beyond their traditional specialization in agricultural and resource exports into trade in manufactures. Exports of manufactures have grown at nearly twice the rate of exports of agriculture and now constitute nearly 80 percent of exports from all developing countries. Countries that were low income in 1980 managed to raise their exports of manufactures from roughly 20 percent of their total exports to more than 80 percent between 1981 and 2001. As a result, many grew quickly and entered the ranks of today's middle-income countries. The middle-income countries of 1980 also increased their manufactured share, but somewhat less rapidly, to reach nearly 70 percent by 2001. This dramatic change in trade magnitudes and composition has given developing countries a new interest—and a powerful voice—in the ongoing Doha Round (World Bank 2003).

One reason for this change was the dramatic reduction in border barriers in developing countries since the mid-1980s, in combination with increased access to markets in rich countries. Because import tariffs indirectly tax exports, reducing trade barriers in developing countries stimulated trade. The burden of import protection on all export activities in developing countries declined, but more for manufactures than for agriculture and natural resources. At the same time, successive multilateral trade rounds liberalized global manufactures, while rich countries continued to protect their agriculture (and developing countries eventually began to follow suit). This state of affairs meant that developing countries' exports of manufactures were free to grow more rapidly than their exports in agriculture.

Today, trade in manufactures is still impeded. Although tariffs on manufacturing in rich countries are on average lower than in developing countries, the tariffs that rich countries charge developing countries are substantially higher than those that they charge industrial countries. For example, exporters of manufactures from industrial countries face, on average, a tariff of 1 percent on their sales to other industrial countries; exporters in developing countries pay anywhere from 2 percent if they are in Latin America (where the North American Free Trade Agreement weighs heavily) to 8 percent if they are in South Asia. Overall, rich countries collect from developing countries about twice the tariff revenues per U.S. dollar of imports that they collect from other rich countries—despite preferential access programs. But the problem is not solely a North-South issue. Latin American exporters of manufactures, for example, face tariffs in neighboring Latin American markets that are seven times higher than the ones they face in industrial countries. In Sub-Saharan Africa, the same multiple is six; in South Asia, two.

Protection takes forms other than tariffs, among them quotas, specific duties, and contingent protection measures such as antidumping duties. As with tariffs, these measures tend to be used more frequently against labor-intensive products from developing countries. The quota arrangements in the WTO Agreement on Textiles and Clothing still shackle the exports of many poor countries. Although these agreements are scheduled to be removed by January 2005, rich countries to date have freed up only 15 percent of trade, obliging them to implement major changes at the end of the phase-in period. Average antidumping duties are seven to ten times higher than tariffs in industrial countries and about five times higher than tariffs in developing countries. Today's protection remains heavily concentrated in the most politically sensitive areas—textiles, clothing, and other labor-intensive manufactures, as well as agriculture—in both rich and poor countries.

Services Liberalization Could Raise Productivity

Services are the fastest-growing component of the global economy. Even in developing countries, service exports grew more rapidly than

manufactures in the 1990s (World Bank 2001). More efficient "back-
bone" services—finance, telecommunications, domestic transportation, retail and wholesale distribution, and professional business
services—improve the performance of the whole economy because
they have broad linkage effects. A large (and ever-increasing) share of
the total costs of production for many firms is services related—as
mentioned, the costs of service inputs are an important determinant
of competitiveness. Competition is the most effective instrument to
lower average costs and increase quality and variety of services. Yet
most developing regions trail the industrial world in exposing service
sectors to competition. Only Latin American countries are beginning
to approximate the high-income countries in their degree of competition (figure 3.9). Estimates suggest that, after controlling for other
determinants of growth, countries that fully liberalized trade and
investment in finance and telecommunications grew on average

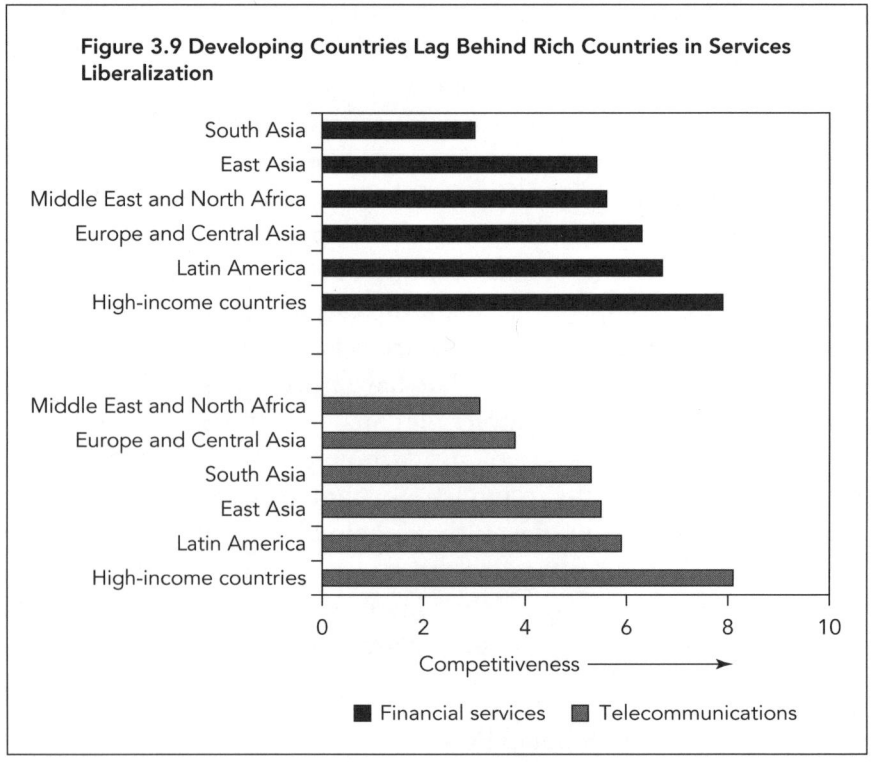

Figure 3.9 Developing Countries Lag Behind Rich Countries in Services Liberalization

Source: World Bank 2001, based on data from Mattoo, Rathindran, and Subramanian 2001.

1.5 percentage points faster than other countries over the past decade (Mattoo, Rathindran, and Subramanian 2001).

No less important, developing countries have an interest in locking in market access for their service exports to markets in rich countries, exports that are growing more rapidly than merchandise exports. Examples include China's incipient software industry and back-office services from India. The Doha Round has the potential of locking in access to foreign markets for services exports. Just as many rich countries have not yet bound access for developing countries' services exports, many developing countries have yet to schedule with the WTO the liberalizing reforms that they have already undertaken. Offers to bind unilateral reforms can be used to lock in existing access to overseas services markets. Active participation in the services negotiations could help accelerate these two processes (Mattoo 2003).

The General Agreement on Trade in Services (GATS) process allows governments to liberalize services at their own pace. It does not require that a government forgo its regulatory responsibilities. Nor does the GATS framework require a cessation of subsidies or preempt propoor regulation on universal service access. The main requirement is that, once a sector is scheduled, governments have in place transparent regulations, treat domestic and foreign companies alike, and permit all foreign companies access to the domestic market on the same terms as domestic companies. In fact, many governments have chosen to liberalize—but not to make commitments through the GATS that would bind them to this opening. Some two-thirds of the WTO members have scheduled fewer than 60 sectors of the approximately 160 sectors covered by the GATS. For example, only 12 developing countries have made commitments in education. None have made commitments in the provision of water.

Why the reluctance? Liberalization in services is more complicated than liberalization in goods markets. Privatization without competition and proper regulation may achieve nothing more than transforming a public monopoly into a private monopoly—with no improvement in services. If the buyer is foreign, the net impact on national welfare may, therefore, be negative. Too many developing countries have been content to change ownership through privatization while retaining limits on entry that buttress monopolies. Thus, procompetitive regulation must be an important complement to privatization and liberalization of access for foreign suppliers.

Effective regulation is also critical to ensure that the poor have access to basic services (World Bank 2002a, 2002b). Some sectors, such as retail and wholesale services, can be opened expeditiously because competition can be relied on to discipline the pricing and investment decisions of firms. But others require well-formulated regulations before liberalization to ensure proper market functioning and adequate access to services for low-income groups. In China's financial sector, for example, the World Bank recommended that financial markets be opened gradually to allow regulations and institutional developments to precede liberalization. The goal was to avoid destabilizing financial losses by state banks that were saddled with poor portfolios as efficient banks, domestic and foreign, entered the market (World Bank 1996). China's WTO accession agreement generally reflected this phased approach. In network sectors, such as telecommunications and water, ensuring adequate pricing and universal access is similarly important if the poor are to benefit from the expansion of the system (World Bank 2001, chapter 3). Trade ministers wishing to harness the reciprocal negotiating framework of the GATS to spur domestic reforms while leveraging market access abroad must ensure that sectoral ministries have appropriate regulation in place to support liberalization.

Singapore Issues: Trade Facilitation Can Have the Biggest Development Effect

A controversial area for negotiations are the so-called Singapore issues—investment and competition policy, transparency in government procurement, and trade facilitation. A virtual consensus emerged in the period after the 2003 WTO ministerial meeting in Cancún that it would not be productive to launch negotiations on the first three issues. Research suggests that from a development perspective this outcome would be good, because, of the four issues, trade facilitation is both important and an area where the WTO can help improve trade opportunities for developing countries. The cost of moving goods across international borders is often as important as formal trade barriers in determining the cost of landed goods—and ultimately of market share. One study estimated that every day spent in customs adds nearly 1 percent to the cost of goods (Hummels 2001). In developing countries, transit costs are routinely two to four times higher than such costs in rich countries. Transparent customs regimes, modern port facilities, dense transportation networks, and access to information and telecommunications systems—all can help lower transit costs.

Facilitating trade by eliminating delays in developing countries would lower trading costs significantly, particularly if this step were accompanied by liberalization of transport and telecommunications and by streamlined regulations to promote domestic competition. Trade facilitation requires modernizing customs, improving port facilities, and making investments in trade-related information technology—a huge institutional and infrastructural agenda. Countries display wide variation in customs efficiency and clearance times (figure 3.10). If countries whose trade-facilitation capacity was below average could be brought halfway up to the global average, international trade would increase by US$380 billion a year (World Bank 2003).

Realizing the Promise of Doha Will Promote Sustainable Growth

Realizing the promise of sustainable growth through international collective actions on the Doha Agenda depends on efforts in agriculture, labor-intensive manufactures, and services. The potential for

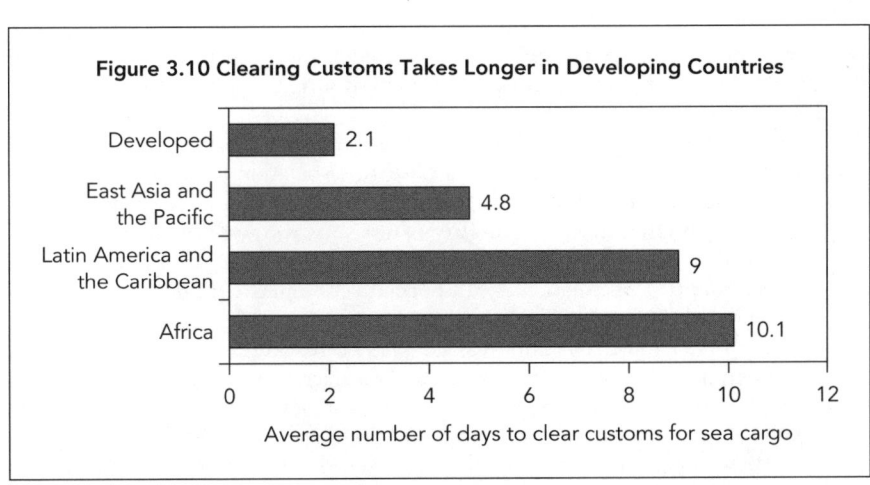

Figure 3.10 Clearing Customs Takes Longer in Developing Countries

Developed — 2.1
East Asia and the Pacific — 4.8
Latin America and the Caribbean — 9
Africa — 10.1

Average number of days to clear customs for sea cargo

Note: Based on a sample of countries in each area.
Source: World Bank 2003.

reciprocal reductions in trade protection holds the promise of better lives for everyone. A recent study considers the effects of a propoor agreement in the Doha Round in which rich countries cut tariff peaks to 10 percent in agriculture and to 5 percent in manufacturing and which is reciprocated in developing countries with cuts to 15 and 10 percent, respectively (World Bank 2003). If these cuts were combined with reductions in prevailing tariff averages, a decoupling of agricultural subsidies from production, and an end to export subsidies, and if they were implemented progressively over the 5 years to 2010, this reform package would produce gains for developing countries of nearly US$350 billion in additional income by 2015 (taking account of the likely productivity response). Rich countries would benefit, too, with gains on the order of US$170 billion.

The outcome would be that 61 million fewer people would be living on less than US$1 a day in 2015, and the number living on less than US$2 a day would be reduced by 140 million.[10] It should be emphasized again that these gains are not guaranteed. Their realization depends on supply-side responses to changed price incentives, and these responses will depend on the investment climate in individual countries, the efficiency of service sectors, and so forth. The numbers illustrate the huge potential that exists for trade to play a role in achieving a major reduction in poverty.

NOTES

1. For contrasting views on the state of the evidence on trade, trade policies, and growth, see Srinivasan and Bhagwati (1999), Rodriguez and Rodrik (1999), and Bernanke and Rogoff (2001).
2. Much of the debate in this area revolves around the policy implications of cross-country regressions that find a positive association between trade (measured by the trade-to-GDP ratio: "openness") and incomes of countries. Critics argue that the direction of causality is not shown by such studies, and that those results are not informative regarding the trade policy stance that accompanies a country's openness ratio. Important econometric studies of the linkage between trade reform and the rate of economic growth include Frankel and Romer (1999) and Sachs and Warner (1995). Rodriguez and Rodrik (1999) is the seminal critique. A recent study by Wacziarg and Welch (2003) addresses a major part of the critique by showing that dates of trade liberalization do characterize breaks in investment and GDP growth rates. Specifically, for the 1950–98 period, countries that liberalized their trade (raising their trade-to-GDP ratio by an average of 5 percentage points) enjoyed on average 1.5 percentage points higher growth in GDP compared with their prereform

rate. See, for example, Baldwin (2003) for a recent survey of the literature and Greenaway, Morgan, and Wright (2002) for a review of the experience of developing countries.

3. Both productivity and variety variables are reported in terms of deviations from their sample means. The regression results control for year and country fixed effects, as well as the endowments differences between countries (Feenstra and Kee 2004a).

4. The impact of FDI on productivity and access to export markets has been incorporated into economic and sectoral work. The 2003 *Slovak Republic Development Policy Review* (World Bank 2002c), 2003 "Lithuania Country Economic Memorandum" (World Bank 2002d), 2004 "Bosnia-Herzegovina Country Economic Memorandum" (World Bank 2004), and Foreign Investment Advisory Service studies (FIAS 2000, 2003) all look at the potential effect of international production and distribution networks associated with inward FDI on export performance productivity. They all have policy recommendations that aim to enhance the scope for positive vertical spillovers (Javorcik Smarzynska and Spatareanu 2003; Javorcik Smarzynska, Saggi, and Spatareanu 2004).

5. The study in question focuses on regulation of new entry (number of procedures and the time and cost involved) and labor-market restrictions on new hiring or layoffs (Bolaky and Freund 2004).

6. The Stolper-Samuelson theorem predicts that an increase in the price of a traded good raises the return to the factor used intensively in the production of the good by a magnitude greater than the initial price increase. Hence, barring structural rigidities, an increase in the price of a labor-intensive good will increase the wage rate by a proportionately higher amount. At the same time, we know that international trade will bring higher prices for the exported commodities—otherwise, domestic firms would have no incentive to produce for the export market. Thus, standard theory suggests that greater participation in labor-intensive trade can reduce poverty by raising the wage rate.

7. This finding, therefore, complements cross-country regression-based analysis such as that of Dollar and Kraay (2001).

8. See Winters (2002) for a survey of the literature.

9. The importance of well-integrated domestic markets for ensuring the effectiveness of trade reforms has been emphasized in the studies of Ethiopia (Integrated Framework 2003) and Mexico (Nicita 2004). Simulation methods have also been used to assess the impact of trade reforms on income distribution and the poor. Examples are model-based analyses for China, the Russian Federation, and Brazil (Gurgel and others 2003) and for the Islamic Republic of Iran (Jensen and Tarr 2002) to assess the effect of alternative types of trade reforms. Results for Russia suggest that virtually all households should gain from the liberalization, with average gains ranging from 2 percent to 25 percent increases in household income. The lack of virtually any losers is explained by the explicit incorporation of services liberalization and endogenous productivity effects (Rutherford and Tarr 2002), two innovative features of this work.

10. *Global Economic Prospects and the Developing Countries 2002* (World Bank 2001) presents illustrations of the gains from services liberalization. Although we do not have firm estimates of relative parameters, several studies have shown that gains are likely to be a multiple of merchandise liberalization. See World Bank (2001), chapter 6.

REFERENCES

Aggarwal, Mita. 1995. "International Trade, Labor Standards, and Labor Market Conditions: An Evaluation of the Linkages." Office of Economics Working Paper 95-06-C. U.S. International Trade Commission, Washington, D.C.

Baldwin, Robert E. 2003. "Openness and Growth: What's the Empirical Relationship?" NBER Working Paper 9578. National Bureau of Economic Research, Cambridge, Mass.

Becker, Randy, and Vernon Henderson. 2000. "Effects of Air Quality Regulation on Polluting Industries." *Journal of Political Economy* 108(2):379–421.

Bernanke, Ben, and Kenneth Rogoff, eds. 2001. *Macroeconomics Annual 2001.* Cambridge, Mass.: MIT Press.

Bolaky, Bineswaree, and Caroline Freund. 2004. "Trade, Regulations, and Growth." World Bank Policy Research Working Paper 3255. Washington, D.C.

Collier, Paul, and David Dollar. Forthcoming. "Globalization: Facts, Fears, and an Agenda for Action." World Bank Policy Research Report, Washington, D.C.

Dollar, David. 1992. "Outward-Oriented Developing Countries Really Do Grow More Rapidly: Evidence from 95 LDCs, 1976–85." *Economic Development and Cultural Change* 40(3):523–44.

Dollar, David, and Aart Kraay. 2001. "Trade, Growth, and Poverty." World Bank Policy Research Working Paper 2199. Washington, D.C.

Elliot, Kimberly Ann. 2001. "Finding Our Way on Trade and Labor Standards." International Economics Policy Briefs. Institute of International Economics, Washington, D.C.

Eskeland, Gunnar, and Ann Harrison. 2003. "Moving to Greener Pastures? Multinationals and the Pollution-Haven Hypothesis." *Journal of Development Economics* 70(1):1–23.

Feenstra, Robert, and Hiau Looi Kee. 2004a. "On the Measurement of Product Variety in Trade." World Bank Policy Research Working Paper 3213. Washington, D.C.

———. 2004b. "Export Variety and Country Productivity." University of California, Davis, and World Bank. Processed.

FIAS (Foreign Investment Advisory Service). 2000. *Evaluation of the Supplier Development Program in the Czech Republic.* Washington, D.C.: World Bank.

———. 2003. *Promoting Knowledge Intensive Industries in Latvia.* Washington, D.C.: World Bank.

Frankel, Jeffrey, and David Romer. 1999. "Does Trade Cause Growth?" *American Economic Review* 89(3):379–99.

Gereffi, Gary, Ronie Garcia-Johnson, and Erika Sasser. 2001. "The NGO-Industrial Complex." *Foreign Policy* (July–August): 56–65.

Greenaway, David, Wyn Morgan, and Peter Wright. 2002. "Trade Liberalisation and Growth in Developing Countries." *Journal of Development Economics* 67(1):229–44.

Grossman, Gene M., and Alan B. Krueger. 1993. "Environmental Impacts of a North American Free Trade Agreement." In Peter M. Garber, ed., *The Mexico-U.S. Free Trade Agreement*. Cambridge, Mass., and London: MIT Press.

Gurgel, Angelo, Glenn Harrison, Thomas Rutherford, and David Tarr. 2003. "Regional, Multilateral, and Unilateral Trade Policies of MERCOSUR for Growth and Poverty Reduction in Brazil." World Bank Policy Research Working Paper 3051. Washington, D.C.

Hallak, Juan Carlos, and James Levinsohn. 2004. "Fooling Ourselves: Evaluating the Globalization and Growth Debate." NBER Working Paper 10244. National Bureau of Economic Research, Cambridge, Mass.

Hoekman, Bernard and Richard Newfarmer. 2003. "After Cancún: Continuation or Collapse?" Trade Note 13. World Bank, Washington, D.C. Available at http://siteresources.worldbank.org/INTRANETTRADE/Resources/Pubs/TradeNote13.pdf.

Hummels, David. 2001. "Time as a Trade Barrier." Department of Economics, Purdue University, Lafayette, Ind. Processed.

Ianchovichina, Elena, Alessandro Nicita, and Isidro Soloaga. 2001. "Trade Reform and Household Welfare: The Case of Mexico." World Bank Policy Research Working Paper 2667. Washington, D.C.

Integrated Framework. 2003. *Ethiopia: Trade and Transformation Challenges*. Diagnostic Trade Integration Study. Available at http://www.integratedframework.org/.

International Monetary Fund and World Bank. 2002. *Market Access for Developing Country Exports: Selected Issues*. Washington, D.C.: World Bank.

Javorcik Smarzynska, Beata. Forthcoming. "Does Foreign Direct Investment Increase the Productivity of Domestic Firms? In Search of Spillovers through Backward Linkages." *American Economic Review*.

Javorcik Smarzynska, Beata, and Mariana Spatareanu. 2003. "To Share or Not to Share: Does Local Participation Matter for Spillovers from Foreign Direct Investment?" World Bank Policy Research Working Paper 3118. Washington, D.C.

Javorcik Smarzynska, Beata, Kamal Saggi, and Mariana Spatareanu. 2004. "Does It Matter Where You Come From? Vertical Spillovers from FDI and Investor's Nationality." World Bank Policy Research Working Paper. Processed.

Jensen, Jesper, and David Tarr. 2002. "Trade, Foreign Exchange, and Energy Policies in the Islamic Republic of Iran: Reform Agenda, Economic Implications, and Impact on the Poor." World Bank Policy Research Working Paper 2768. Washington, D.C.

Keller, Wolfgang, and Arik Levinson. 2002. "Pollution Abatement Costs and Foreign Direct Investment to U.S. States." *Review of Economics and Statistics* 84(4):691–703.

Leonard, H. Jeffrey. 1988. *Pollution and the Struggle for World Product*. Cambridge, U.K.: Cambridge University Press.

Levinson, Arik. 1996. "Environmental Regulation and Manufacturers' Location Choices: Evidence from the Census of Manufactures." *Journal of Public Economics* 62:5–29.

Lindert, Peter, and Jeffrey Williamson. 2001. "Globalization and Inequality: A Long History." Paper presented at the World Bank Annual Bank Conference on Development Economics—Europe, Barcelona, Spain, June 25–27.

Mattoo, Aaditya. 2003. "Services in a Development Round." Paper presented to the OECD Global Forum on Trade, Paris, June 5–6.

Mattoo, Aaditya, Randeep Rathindran, and Arvind Subramanian. 2001. "Measuring Services Trade Liberalization and Its Impact on Economic Growth: An Illustration." World Bank Policy Research Working Paper 2655. Washington, D.C.

Muendler, Marc-Andreas. 2004. "Trade, Technology, and Productivity: A Study of Brazilian Manufacturers, 1986–1998." University of California, San Diego. Processed.

Newfarmer, Richard. 2003. "From Singapore to Cancún: Investment." Trade Note 2. World Bank, Washington, D.C. Available at http://siteresources. worldbank.org/INTRANETTRADE/Resources/TradeNote2.pdf.

Nicita, Alessandro. 2004. "Who Benefited from Trade Liberalization in Mexico? Measuring the Effects on Household Welfare." World Bank Policy Research Working Paper 3265. Washington, D.C.

Nicita, Alessandro, and Marcelo Olarreaga. 2003. "Trade Policy Reform and Poverty in Ethiopia." Processed.

OECD (Organisation for Economic Co-operation and Development). 1996. *Trade, Employment, and Labor Standards: A Study of Core Workers' Rights and International Trade*. Paris.

Pananagariya, Arvind. 1999. "Labor Standards in the WTO and Developing Countries: Trading Rights at Risk." University of Maryland, College Park. Processed.

Pearson, C. 1987. *Multinational Corporation, the Environment, and Development*. Washington, D.C.: World Resources Institute.

Porto, Guido. 2003a. "Using Survey Data to Assess the Distributional Effects of Trade Policy." World Bank Policy Research Working Paper 3137. Washington, D.C.

———. 2003b. "Trade Reforms, Market Access, and Poverty in Argentina." World Bank Policy Research Working Paper 3135. Washington, D.C.

Ravallion, Martin. 1997. "Can High-Inequality Countries Escape Absolute Poverty?" *Economics Letters* 56:151–57.

Rodriguez, Francisco, and Dani Rodrik. 1999. "Trade Policy and Economic Growth: A Skeptic's Guide to the Cross-National Evidence." NBER Working Paper 7081. National Bureau of Economic Research, Cambridge, Mass.

Rutherford, Thomas, and David Tarr. 2002. "Trade Liberalization, Product Variety, and Trade in a Small Open Economy: A Quantitative Assessment." *Journal of International Economics* 56(2):247–72.

Sachs, Jeffrey, and Andrew Warner. 1995. "Economic Convergence and Economic Policies." NBER Working Paper 5039. National Bureau of Economic Research, Cambridge, Mass.

Schiff, Maurice and Yanling Wang. 2003. "NAFTA, Technology Diffusion, and Productivity in Mexico." *Cuadernos de Economia* 40(121):469–76.

_____. 2004. "Education, Governance and Trade-Related Technology Diffusion in Latin America." IZA Working Paper 1028. Forschungsinstitut zur Zukunft der Arbeit, Bonn, Germany.

Schiff, Maurice, Marcelo Olarreaga, and Yanling Wang. 2002. "Trade-Related Technology Diffusion and the Dynamics of North-South and South-South Integration." World Bank Policy Research Working Paper 2861. Washington, D.C.

Srinivasan, T. N., and Jagdish Bhagwati. 1999. "Outward-Orientation and Development: Are Revisionists Right?" Yale University Economic Growth Center Discussion Paper 806. New Haven, Conn.

Tobey, James A. 1990. "The Effects of Domestic Environmental Policies." *Kyklos* 43(2):191–209.

Torres, Raymond. 1996. "Labor Standards and International Trade." *OECD Observer* 202:10–13

Wacziarg, Roman, and Karen Welch. 2003. "Trade Liberalization and Growth: New Evidence." NBER Working Paper 10152. National Bureau of Economic Research, Cambridge, Mass.

Wilson, John S., Mirvat Sewadeh, and Tsunehiro Otsuki. 2001. "Dirty Exports and Environmental Regulation: Do Standards Matter?" World Bank, Washington, D.C. Processed.

Winters, L. Alan. 2002. "Trade Liberalisation and Poverty: What Are the Links?" *World Economy* 25(9):1339–67.

World Bank. 1996. "The Chinese Economy: Fighting Inflation, Deepening Reforms." Washington, D.C.

_____. 2001. *Global Economic Prospects and the Developing Countries 2002: Making Trade Work for the World's Poor.* Washington, D.C.

_____. 2002a. *Global Economic Prospects and the Developing Countries 2003: Investing to Unlock Global Opportunities.* Washington, D.C.

_____. 2002b. *World Development Report 2003: Sustainable Development in a Dynamic World.* Washington, D.C.

_____. 2002c. *Slovak Republic Development Policy Review.* Washington, D.C.

_____. 2002d. "Lithuania Country Economic Memorandum: Converging to Europe: Policies to Support Employment and Productivity Growth." Washington, D.C.

_____. 2003. *Global Economic Prospects and the Developing Countries 2004: Realizing the Development Promise of the Doha Agenda.* Washington, D.C.

_____. 2004. "Bosnia-Herzegovina Country Economic Memorandum." Washington, D.C.

Xu, Xinpeng. 1999. *International Trade and Environmental Regulation: A Dynamic Perspective.* Commack, N.Y.: Nova Science.

CHAPTER 4

TOWARD A SUSTAINABLE
ENERGY FUTURE

Bringing modern energy services to the energy poor—to the 1.6 billion people who lack access to electricity and the 2.4 billion who rely on biomass for cooking and heating—is a major challenge. The majority of those who are underserved are the poor in Sub-Saharan Africa and India. Although the share of people who lack access to electricity and modern fuels is expected to decline, population growth—most of it in urban areas in the developing world—will mean that 1.4 billion people will still lack electricity in 2030. And barring any major policy shifts, 2.6 billion people will continue to rely on biomass in 2030. Lack of access to modern fuels will consign those people to a vicious cycle of poverty, as they will lack the means to afford and attain services essential for increased income, better health, and education.

Changes in cost, technology, availability, and desirability will influence the future use of fuels. Oil is expected to remain dominant, accounting for just under 40 percent of fuel use to 2025. Natural gas is expected to be a fast-growing source of primary energy until 2025, increasing from 23 percent in 2001 to 28 percent in 2025, while coal use is expected to decline from 24 percent to 22 percent of world energy consumption (Energy Information Agency 2003, p. 3). China, India, and some other parts of developing Asia that are home

This chapter builds on the World Bank's Energy Strategy and is a collaborative effort, with contributions by Jamal Saghir, Elizabeth Kelley, Gary Stuggins, and Kyran O'Sullivan of the Energy and Water Department.

to significant coal deposits are expected to rely more on coal. A decline in the use of nuclear power, from 19 percent to 12 percent, is expected as older plants are retired and public concerns about safety and environmental issues remain. And reliance on renewable resources is expected to grow at an average annual rate of 1.9 percent. Much of this increase will be due to large hydropower projects, because most renewable technologies, in the absence of major investments in research and development, are not expected to be cost-competitive with fossil fuels in the coming decades. Renewable technologies will be much more cost-competitive if fossil fuel subsidies are eliminated and if environmental spillovers are figured into energy prices.

What are the implications of these projected shifts in fuel use? Given the overall increase in energy demand predicted for the next two decades—an estimated annual average growth rate of 2.4 percent for electricity alone—environmental concerns are likely to be significant. Increasing the primary energy supply will require the development of more marginal resources, thus increasing the cost of supply. Attracting the investments to increase capacity and meet growing demand—along with implementing strong measures to increase energy efficiency—will also be vital.

ENERGY'S ROLE IN RESPONSIBLE GROWTH—THE MULTIPLIER EFFECT OF MODERN ENERGY

Energy services are an essential part of responsible growth, extending well beyond the direct uses of energy services—heating, cooking, and lighting—to a range of essential building blocks of development. Electric lighting for schools and homes allows students to read beyond daylight hours or in spaces where natural lighting is limited. Households that have modern energy services for cooking and lighting are spared the chore of collecting wood and other biomass for those needs—a chore that can consume hours of productive time for women and children. Relieved of this burden, children are afforded more time for attending school, and women can devote more time to agriculture and other productive activities—which can in turn provide income to cover the cost of the energy services.

The correlations between modern energy services and environmental health are also significant, particularly for the 2.4 billion people in developing countries who rely on biomass for cooking and heating. Indoor air pollution from cooking with biomass and charcoal in traditional stoves is a major cause of acute respiratory illness. According to the World Health Organization, 2.5 million women and children in developing countries die prematurely each year from breathing polluted air generated by traditional cooking stoves used indoors. The benefits of shifting to more modern energy services for cooking are well proven—substituting liquefied petroleum gas for wood in cooking can reduce the overall health risk by a factor of more than 100 (International Energy Agency 2003, "Energy and Poverty" chapter). Modern energy is required for refrigeration, which delays spoiling of food and allows for safe storage of medicines, and for pumping and purifying groundwater, which is essential for health and agriculture.

Responsible growth cannot be achieved without the basic building blocks of education, health, clean drinking water, and opportunity to pursue productive activities. Although large enterprises in developing countries can often afford backup generators or independent methods for power production, small and medium-size enterprises are generally limited to grid energy services, which may not be available or reliable. When modern energy, a key component of productivity, is not widely available and reliable, the economy faces a major hurdle on the path to growth and expansion. From the household level up to the level of a large corporation, modern energy services are essential for increasing productivity and bringing the benefits of modern technology.

Urbanization and Population Growth

Global population is expected to grow from 6 billion in 2000 to more than 9 billion in 2050, with 95 percent of this growth in the urban developing world. This growth will require a major shift in strategy for bringing energy to the unserved (four of five people without access to energy today live in rural areas). Safe, affordable energy services will be essential for the megacities of the future, yet rural areas cannot be neglected. Aside from the imperative of supplying the rural poor, providing energy services for economic opportunities in rural areas could also help reduce mass migration to urban areas, thereby easing the strain on infrastructure in big cities.

The plight of the urban poor, especially those in the slums of such megacities as Lagos and Cairo, will require significant attention to energy services. The poorest urban dwellers in such megacities often have no access to modern energy or clean water and must forage among the detritus of the slums for materials with which to cook and heat their homes. Living standards of urban dwellers can drop even below those of the rural poor when unemployment is high, productive activities are scarce, and income is very low. Slum dwellers, who are not even able to grow food on the scarce land and who are distant from forests or other sources of biomass, are left with only trash for heating and cooking or illegal, risky, and unreliable connections to power lines.

The urban poor present a new challenge for energy policymakers; although they are concentrated and, thus, easier and less expensive to reach and connect to the grid, their purchasing power and economic opportunities are often very limited. By addressing those two issues in concert with energy-specific approaches, energy interventions can have a much greater and longer-lasting effect.

Environmental Concerns

Recent environmental public opinion surveys conducted by Globe-Scan in 20 countries concluded, "Environmental concerns in poor and middle-income countries are clearly linked to personal perceived risks and basic needs, while in wealthy countries people are beginning to put nature issues ahead of their historical pollution concerns" (GlobeScan 2003). The environment and poor people who rely heavily on the natural environment are often the victims of unsound energy practices. Household and urban air pollution are rampant in developing countries, where affordability is the driving factor for energy decisions. This problem is compounded by the fact that developing countries have fewer environmental regulations in place than do industrial countries. Those who suffer the most from the consequences of environmental harm are often the poor, who depend heavily on the products of forests, rivers, and lakes for their livelihoods.

ENERGY AS A DRIVER OF RESPONSIBLE GROWTH

Providing the energy needed to maintain and expand living standards and economic prosperity will be one of the biggest challenges of the twenty-first century. The reference scenario of the International Energy Agency (2002) projects continuing rapid growth in energy demand from now until 2030, at a rate of 1.7 percent annually. By 2030, the world will be consuming two-thirds more energy than it is today. And developing countries will replace the industrial world as the largest group of energy consumers. Fossil fuels are forecast to remain the dominant sources of energy and will provide more than 90 percent of the coming increase in demand.

The path that energy growth will take in the future will depend on many factors, including population levels; economic output; the structures of the world's economies; resource availability; the development and deployment of improved technologies for producing, transforming, and consuming energy; and government energy, economic, and environmental policies. Achieving progress in modernizing energy can have a major effect on achieving higher rates of responsible growth. Energy is essential in achieving poverty reduction objectives because it is fundamental to increasing labor productivity.

Low-income countries typically have a very large proportion of the population working in the agriculture sector. Through productivity gains, human resources can be freed up to pursue developmental objectives and to increase the creation of wealth. Energy can fuel mechanical equipment for agricultural activities, including production, transformation, and transportation. It can release time spent gathering fuel for productive use. It can power small and medium-size enterprises. And it can facilitate communications over telephones, television, radio, and computer networks.

Applying modern energy can improve crop yields (through mechanized equipment), extend preservation of foods to longer periods, and allow foods to be transported to markets more quickly and efficiently. Providing access to universal primary education and providing equal access for girls are linked to the improved lighting that modern energy affords.

Energy is also key to reducing the deaths of children under 5 years old and of mothers. Deaths at birth can be reduced by proper lighting and clean, boiled water. Deaths from diarrhea, which kills 2 million to 3 million children each year, can also be reduced through clean, boiled water (which requires energy both for extraction and for heating). Illness and death from indoor air pollution can be reduced through use of cleaner-burning fuels and modern stoves and hearths. Deaths from hunger can be reduced by access to fuels needed to improve production, to increase the effectiveness of transportation of products, and to cook staple foods, such as rice and wheat, on which the poor depend.

Halting the spread of major diseases also requires energy to refrigerate and store medicines and vaccines, to provide lighting for treatment centers, and to enable modern communications for delivering information on primary health and updating doctors. Modern energy's contribution to protecting the environment is realized by improving the local environment in the household, by reducing land degradation from unsustainable fuel gathering, and by easing local ambient pollution, especially in cities.

IMPROVEMENTS TO ENERGY EFFICIENCY

One of the most promising aspects of a sustainable energy future, provided that sufficient investment in research and development exists, is the potential for technological innovations in energy efficiency, renewables, and advanced fossil fuel development. The savings that can be achieved through implementation of energy efficiency measures are great: one estimate by the Energy Policy Research Institute shows that a US$4.2 billion annual investment in energy efficiency would reduce U.S. peak demand by 45,000 megawatts; the cost of building new generation capacity of 45,000 megawatts would be US$8.5 billion (Energy Future Coalition 2003). Furthermore, projections for the cost-effective reduction in primary energy inputs for a given level of energy services are 40 percent for transition economies and 45 percent for developing countries in the next 20 years (Turkenburg and Faaij 2000, p. 13). The challenge is to make these energy-saving investments attractive, affordable (upfront capital costs can be prohibitive), and widespread.

Energy intensity—the amount of energy consumed per unit of gross domestic product (GDP)—is a useful indicator of how efficiently an economy uses energy. It tends to decline once an economy reaches a mature industrial stage and transitions to a service economy. Existing industrial capacity, greater efficiency of modern energy over traditional energy, and greater efficiency in energy service delivery and end use all reduce the need for additional energy for economic growth.

Developing economies generally have higher energy intensities, largely because the shift from an agricultural to an industrial economy requires significant increases in energy use. Historical trends show that, as a growing economy shifts to an industrial structure, as the fuel mix transitions from traditional to modern fuels such as electricity, and as end use becomes more streamlined and efficient, energy intensity falls—at historical rates of between 1 percent and 1.5 percent a year (carbon intensity declines at only 0.3 percent to 0.4 percent a year). This decline is steepest in transition economies as the structure of the economy changes, as more efficient energy practices are adopted, and as more advanced energy technologies come into use as new industries evolve.

The outlook for energy intensity in the coming decades, though uncertain, shows a worldwide decline. So although economic growth will undoubtedly be accompanied by increased demand for energy, the rate of growth in energy demand relative to economic growth may decline. Widespread implementation of energy-efficiency measures—including through technology transfer from advanced economies—can slow this rate even further. Indeed, more efficient technologies can allow developing countries to grow using less energy than industrial countries did at a comparable stage of development.

ENERGY CONSUMPTION—THE DOWNSIDE OF GROWTH?

Energy intensity increases when economies first industrialize. Thereafter energy intensity declines with growth, and per capita consumption of energy tends to rise with income. In 1995, average per capita consumption of energy in the United States was more than eight times that in Sub-Saharan Africa. This disparity is due to many factors. An industrial economy will logically have far higher per capita energy consumption than an agrarian one, but the affordability of energy and the lack of incentive to conserve energy widen this gap.

Although efficiency gains that are due to improved technologies will help curb energy demand, conservation among end users and incentives to develop and implement efficient technologies are important elements of a sustainable energy future.

ENERGY PRICING AND AFFORDABILITY

One of the greatest obstacles for both energy policymakers and the poor is proper pricing of modern energy services. In many countries—both developing and industrial—energy prices (whether for electricity, oil, gas, or other fuels) do not reflect the cost of that fuel. Even more rarely do energy prices reflect the economic cost of the use of that fuel. From the perspective of the poor, the costs of modern energy services often represent a significant proportion of income, and where biomass is "free" and abundant, affordability questions are more complex. It is often difficult or impossible for a poor rural family to afford a connection to the electric grid—which can run into the hundreds of dollars—or to afford the bottles and other startup costs for liquefied petroleum gas or kerosene. Even after the service connection is established, the cost of energy usage can be a major drain on the household budget. Lack of credit for the poor exacerbates this problem, as many poor households do not have a steady income and can easily fall into arrears on bills.

Subsidies can help bridge the gap between what poor consumers can afford and the cost of the connection or service. But the inefficiencies associated with subsidies make this policy option complicated. Subsidies to cover part of the capital cost of service connection can help with extending electricity to unserved households, but the high cost of the connection can be burdensome for governments facing a shortage of cash. Lifeline tariffs provide another alternative for helping poor households maintain a service connection by providing a limited quantity of electricity, natural gas, or district heating at low cost.

Determining the correct subsidy can be challenging, and some countries set the consumption threshold for lifeline rates so high that they benefit wealthy consumers more than the poor. If the cost of new connections can be subsidized to some extent, poor households will more readily be able to afford services.

For the policymaker and energy service provider, cost recovery is an ongoing challenge. In many countries with poor sector governance, theft of electricity is rampant; the *World Energy Outlook* (International Energy Agency 2002) found that up to a third of all power produced in India is stolen. Compared with mere technical losses in member countries of the Organisation for Economic Co-operation and Development (on the order of 5 percent), those losses are not only remarkable, but also very costly for the utilities. Setting tariffs at cost recovery levels is also a challenge, given the high subsidies to which consumers in many transitional and some developing countries are accustomed. During the Soviet era, consumers paid very low tariffs for electricity, heating, and cooking fuels, and the price increases that have accompanied reform have been difficult for the poor.

Externalities—such as the environmental and health costs borne by society as a whole—often do not appear on the operators' balance sheets. Many commercially proven, nonpolluting technologies, including renewable energy technologies, are thereby at a disadvantage because of implicit subsidies on competing fuels and technologies. The levels of subsidies for the fossil fuel and nuclear industries are very high in the European Union and elsewhere. Those subsidies seriously distort markets for generated energy, hence hurting the ability of commercial renewable technologies to compete.

If countries are to take full advantage of their renewable energy resources, they need support to overcome financing constraints, to improve technical and institutional capacities, and to remove policy constraints and regulatory bottlenecks. Some forms of renewable energy are not economical today, but they have considerable potential should their costs decline and their performance improve.

FINANCIAL SUSTAINABILITY AND INVESTMENT NEEDS

Private foreign energy investment in developing and transitional economies peaked in 1997 at close to US$51 billion. It then dropped off because of the emerging markets crisis. Later it recovered somewhat, but it then dropped again to US$7 billion in 2002 in the wake of the global economic downturn and the Enron scandal.

The investment needs are enormous. For the power sector, annual investments in developing and transitional economies will have to rise from US$120 billion in 2002 to US$175 billion in 2020 with 2 percent growth and to US$210 billion with 3 percent growth (figure 4.1). For electricity-generating capacity alone, US$3.1 trillion will be needed for developing countries and US$400 billion for transitional economies through 2030 (International Energy Agency 2002, p. 71). For transmission and distribution capacity, the investment needs are similar. Given that overseas development assistance from industrial to developing countries declined in the 1990s, the financing gap looms even larger.

How can the investment gap be overcome? Clearly, the climate for investment must be healthy and the risks predictable if the private sector is to reengage in the energy sector. Different risk allocation regimes will also be necessary, making use of concessions, leasing arrangements, and management contracts to increase private sector participation. In a recent survey of energy investors, adequate retail prices and stability and enforcement of laws and contracts ranked

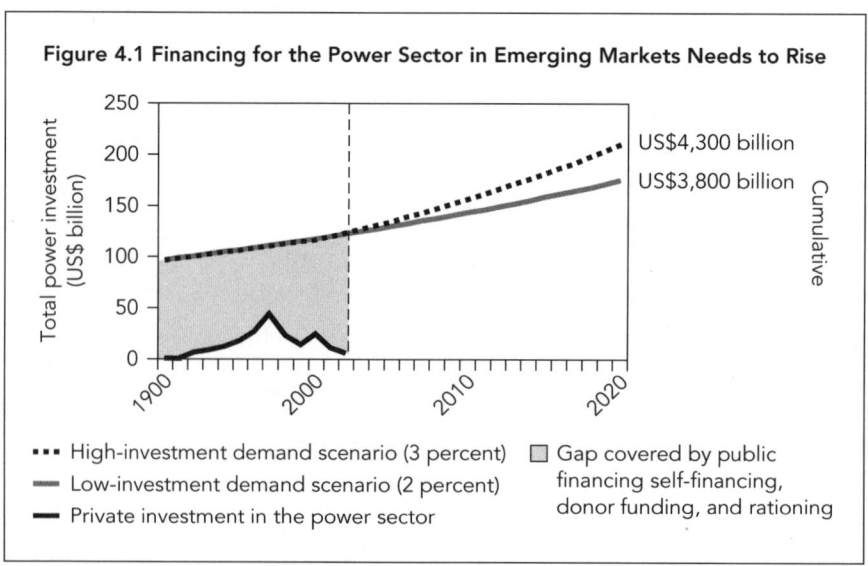

Figure 4.1 Financing for the Power Sector in Emerging Markets Needs to Rise

US$4,300 billion
US$3,800 billion

••• High-investment demand scenario (3 percent)
— Low-investment demand scenario (2 percent)
— Private investment in the power sector

☐ Gap covered by public financing self-financing, donor funding, and rationing

Source: World Bank, IEA, Deloitte Touche Tohmatsu Emerging Markets Group 2004.

high among the priority issues for investors considering entry into a market. Yet those elements are often lacking in developing countries that have newly liberalized energy markets.

Without market reforms and solid regulatory structures, the energy sector in middle-income countries will continue to suffer from underinvestment. Guidance on legal and regulatory reform for developing countries and guarantees for investors can help limit risks, render the sector more transparent, and increase its attractiveness to investors. In poor countries in Sub-Saharan Africa, a framework for sustained development assistance will be needed.

FISCAL BURDENS ON CASH-STRAPPED GOVERNMENTS

Domestic governments often sustain or even administer energy services. Even where the utility is not state run, the combined effect of subsidies and other aid makes the state a significant player, with quasi-fiscal deficits of as high as 10 percent of GDP for the energy service sectors of some countries.

High oil prices in poor oil-importing countries can make the oil import bill so huge that it provokes a fiscal crisis. The recent worldwide drop in private investment and the stress on government budgets have reduced the options for financing attainable in the near term to make needed upgrades and expand networks.

FOUR STRATEGIES FOR ENERGY

The 2002 World Summit on Sustainable Development, held in Johannesburg, renewed international attention to the critical role of energy in sustainable development. Energy issues formed a significant element in the summit's negotiations and outcomes. And indeed, energy returned to the top of the international development agenda. The summit commitments stressed the need for broadening access to energy, for increasing reliance on renewable energy resources, for removing market distortions, for improving the targeting of subsidies, and for establishing energy-efficiency programs. Although the summit did not agree to any targets or timetables regarding energy commitments, it provided a wakeup call for policymakers and the public to address the energy challenge.

Substantial progress toward the summit's energy objectives will require coordinated efforts and significant political commitments from multilateral development institutions and from governments. Some countries are well on track to delivering modern energy services, to increasing energy efficiency, and to improving the functioning and transparency of energy markets. But others—particularly in Sub-Saharan Africa—are woefully behind. A coordinated multilateral approach is needed to help countries break out of the energy poverty trap, protect shared natural resources, and move toward a sustainable energy future.

Helping the Poor Directly

Developing countries need to increase poor people's access to modern fuels and electricity. Doing so involves reducing the costs and improving the quality of energy supplied to the poor, as well as ensuring that energy subsidies are targeted to and reach the poor. Health issues deserve attention as well, in efforts to promote energy-efficient and less polluting end-use technologies for traditional fuels. Such efforts can include providing more efficient stoves with proper ventilation for poor households that rely on biomass for cooking and heating or replacing traditional stoves with those that use modern liquid fuels.

The economic stimulus that modern energy can provide is encouraged through efforts to create energy service enterprises run by the poor (box 4.1). When energy services are commercialized, rural entrepreneurs can benefit from the new economic activity in their community by joining the ranks of service providers. This opportunity provides both income-generating possibilities as well as a sense of local ownership.

Finally, energy programs should work cross-sectorally by supporting energy provision for social services, including education, communication, and health. Recognizing the vital role of energy in those services and integrating those sectors into energy projects ensures that the benefits of energy services reach beyond their direct and immediate applications of cooking, heating, and lighting.

Box 4.1   The Community Development Carbon Fund

The World Bank, in collaboration with the International Emissions Trading Association, has created a new fund to provide carbon finance through the Clean Development Mechanism. The Community Development Carbon Fund links small-scale projects seeking carbon finance with companies, governments, foundations, and nongovernmental organizations seeking to improve the livelihoods of local communities and obtain verified emission reductions.

Contributors to the fund support projects that measurably benefit the poor and will receive emission reductions from abated or sequestered emissions. These "Development + Carbon" emission reductions (emission reductions with the added value of development benefits) have the potential to be recognized under emerging global, national, and regional programs.

The Community Development Carbon Fund is a public-private initiative established as a trust fund, similar to the Prototype Carbon Fund. The target size is US$100 million. An advisory group of outside experts helped design the fund, which mobilizes parallel resources from donors to support technical assistance and project preparation.

Improving Macroeconomic and Fiscal Stability

The macroeconomic and fiscal aspects of the energy sector demand stability. Rationalizing quasi-fiscal deficits and energy taxes is one key element in stability, because it will free resources that can be allocated to health and education services for the poor. Replacing public investments with private ones can also relieve a major strain on national budgets, while increasing investment possibilities and bringing needed financing to the energy sector.

Contingent public liabilities can pose risks for governments, so governments need help in managing those risks better. By assisting countries in closing loss-making coal mines and oil refineries and by financing restructuring costs that fall on government budgets, donors can ensure that fiscal stability will not fall victim to domestic energy sector shifts.

Subsidies often constitute a major drain on national budgets, sometimes unnecessarily so. By working to enhance commercialization within the sector, including payment by all energy users, countries can eliminate operating subsidies to state-owned enterprises, thereby reducing the budget strain. They can also target subsidies more effectively.

Countries that rely on imported energy services can benefit from more efficient procurement to lower costs. And exporting countries can benefit from techniques for better marketing, thereby increasing revenues. They can also improve the governance of export revenues and possibly sequester surpluses to ensure that corruption is curtailed and the proceeds are used wisely.

Promoting Good Governance and Private Sector Development

The Enron-type scandals of recent years brought to light the challenges of good governance and the dangers of corruption in the energy sector. Private enterprises, even in the wealthiest countries, are not immune to issues of poor governance. The recent corporate scandals have provided lessons for developing countries in how to establish an environment in which good governance is the norm and the private sector can flourish. That is why developing countries need help in creating objective, transparent, nondiscriminatory regulatory mechanisms. They need to expand competition and cross-border trade in energy services and resources. And they need to divest assets to strategic investors in regulated markets in a socially responsible and corruption-free way.

Countries are attracting private investment by liberalizing entry into energy markets. They are also considering effects at the local level, thus strengthening the voices of consumers and communities— those most affected by energy price shifts and interruptions. And they are trying to strengthen local financing institutions so that they can provide long-term financing to rural energy businesses for more employment opportunities and local ownership.

Protecting the Environment through Energy Choices

New renewable energy sources and other clean technologies, which are considered by some as the logical energy choice of the future, do not yet contribute a significant portion of total world energy supply. On a longer time horizon, their potential is great. Wind, solar (photovoltaic and thermal), and marine power now account for less than 2 percent of the world's energy demand, while all renewables, including hydropower and traditional biomass, account for 14 percent of world energy demand. Without major policy shifts in favor of renewables, prospects are limited. Both wind and photovoltaic power are growing rapidly, but they will remain a small portion of total supply.

Small hydro, solar, wind, geothermal, biomass, and district heating are all part of the effort to promote and support sustainable development. The World Bank Group has actively supported renewable energy development, with cumulative commitments of about US$2.7 billion in direct investments plus leveraged foreign and domestic investments through Multilateral Investment Guarantee Agency guarantees and Carbon Finance Business in 72 projects in 36 countries. Those commitments account for 14 percent of the World Bank's energy portfolio, up from 4 percent in 1990. Many of the investments are jointly supported by the Global Environment Facility, Prototype Carbon Fund, or Community Development Carbon Fund. To further scale up investments in support of the Infrastructure Action Plan, the World Bank is vigorously pursuing wide-ranging consultations—both internally and with bilateral and multilateral partners.

JOINT EFFORTS NEEDED

Partnering with governments, public institutions, and the private sector is essential for ensuring the sustainability of energy investments. The contribution of renewable, environmentally friendly energy sources can grow, but only in the framework of prudent, economically sound policies implemented by governments. Incremental financing sources from public institutions, coupled with technological innovation and operational support from the private sector, can help governments deliver energy services. By working to improve the climate for investment in the energy sector, developing countries aim to increase the contribution of the private sector and to relieve governments of some of the burden of new investments.

Progress on efficiency measures also requires joint efforts and strong commitment. The potential for energy savings through efficiency investments and changes in end-user behavior is significant, but the incentives must be made clear and barriers removed. By raising awareness of the need to conserve and by sharing information about the benefits of energy efficiency, the World Bank and the broader development community aim to spur action on the part of both client countries and member countries of the Organisation for Economic Co-operation and Development.

Finally, flexibility in approaching the energy challenge is key. If we are to address the challenge successfully and reduce the ranks of the energy poor, we must adapt to new challenges quickly while taking advantage of the possibilities of new technologies. Through a strong commitment to partnership, innovation, and flexibility, we can forge a sustainable energy future.

REFERENCES

Deloitte Emerging Markets Group. 2004. "Sustainable Power Sector Reform in Emerging Markets—Financial Issues and Options: Joint World Bank/USAID Policy Paper." Washington, D.C.

Energy Future Coalition. 2003. "Challenge and Opportunity: Charting a New Energy Future." Washington, D.C. Available at http://www.energyfuturecoalition.org/full_report/index.shtm.

Energy Information Agency. 2003. *International Energy Outlook*. Washington, D.C.

GlobeScan. 2003. "International Environmental Monitor." Toronto, Canada. Available at http://www.GlobeScan.com.

International Energy Agency. 2002. *World Energy Outlook 2002*. Paris.

Turkenburg, Wim C., and André P. C. Faaij. 2000. "World Energy Assessment: Energy and the Challenge of Sustainability." Department of Science, Technology and Society, Utrecht University, Utrecht, Netherlands.

World Energy Council. 2002. "Global Energy Report: Energy and Sustainable Development." London.

CHAPTER 5

WATER RESOURCES: MANAGING SCARCITY

The World Commission on Water has described the "gloomy arithmetic of water" (World Commission on Water 2000). During the past century, while world population tripled, the use of water increased sixfold. Irrigation now accounts for 70 percent of global water withdrawals, industry for 20 percent, and municipal use for 10 percent. The increased use of water has come at high environmental costs. Some rivers no longer reach the sea. Half of the world's wetlands have disappeared in the past century. A fifth of freshwater fish are endangered or extinct. And many of the most important groundwater aquifers are being mined, with water tables already deep and dropping by meters every year, and some damaged permanently by salinization.

The World Commission on Water estimates that water use will increase by about 50 percent in the next 30 years. An estimated 4 billion people—half of the world's population—will live under conditions of severe water stress in 2025, with conditions particularly severe in Africa, the Middle East, and South Asia. Compounding the relative scarcity of water is the continuous deterioration in water quality in most developing countries. And it is the poorest countries and poorest people who are most directly affected.

This gloomy arithmetic of water is mirrored in the gloomy arithmetic of costs. Although low-cost, often community-based solutions

This chapter builds on the World Bank's Water Resources Strategy (World Bank 2004) and was prepared by John Briscoe of the Agriculture and Rural Department.

can be further tapped, the "easy and cheap" options for mobilizing additional major sources of supply for human needs have mostly been exploited. Many countries are now facing sharply increasing unit costs (often associated with interbasin transfers or desalination).

Population and economic growth, plus greater appreciation of the value of water in ecosystems, means that water demands are growing and shifting. Tensions over water rights are increasing at the level of the village, city, and basin. Some of those disputes are spilling over to international river basins. Shifting patterns of precipitation and runoff associated with climate change compound this gloomy arithmetic. An inability to predict and manage the quantity and quality of water and the impacts of droughts, floods, and climatic variability imposes large costs on many economies in the developing world. If the computer simulations on climate change are correct, those impacts will only heighten in the coming decades.

All countries thus face major challenges in developing the laws, regulations, and institutions to manage water resources in ways that are economically productive, socially acceptable, and environmentally sustainable. Better resource and demand management, therefore, has a high priority. The details have to be tailored to the historical, cultural, environmental, social, economic, and political circumstances of each country.

And all countries face a major challenge in developing and maintaining an appropriate stock of water infrastructure, including dikes, canals, dams, and interbasin transfers. Industrial countries have largely completed their investments in major water infrastructure, but developing countries have not. Europe and North America have developed 75 percent of their potential, whereas Africa has developed only less than 7 percent. Australia and Ethiopia have similar degrees of climatic variability, but Australia has 5,000 cubic meters of water storage capacity per person and Ethiopia 45 cubic meters. The United States and Nepal have roughly equivalent economically exploitable hydropower potential. Installed hydropower capacity in the United States is about 70,000 megawatts—in Nepal it is fewer than 600 megawatts.

Infrastructure-rich industrial countries should focus appropriately on management reforms. Developing countries must simultaneously improve the way they manage water and water services—and invest in priority infrastructure.

NECESSITY OF WATER MANAGEMENT AND DEVELOPMENT FOR GROWTH AND POVERTY REDUCTION

Effective water resource development and ecological management play a fundamental role in sustainable growth and poverty reduction, through four different mechanisms (table 5.1). First, broad-based water resource interventions (type 1), usually including major infrastructure such as dams and interbasin transfers, provide national, regional, and local benefits from which all people, including the poor, can gain. Second, because it is usually the poor who inhabit degraded landscapes, poverty-targeted water resource interventions designed to improve catchment quality and provide livelihoods for the poor (type 2) are of major importance. Third, broad-based water service interventions (type 3), aimed at improving the performance of utilities, user associations, and irrigation departments, benefit everyone, including the poor. And fourth, poverty-targeted water service interventions (type 4), such as water and sanitation and irrigation services for the unserved poor, play a major role in improving the lives of the poor.

In most developing countries, growth-oriented, poverty-reducing water resource strategies will involve action in all four areas. The corollary is that donors must be available as full-service partners to assist development of integrated and consistent action in all four areas.

Table 5.1 A Typology of Water Interventions

	Broad interventions	Poverty-targeted interventions
Interventions affecting water resources, development, and management	*Type 1:* Broad regionwide water resource interventions (for example, multipurpose river basin development and aquifer management)	*Type 2:* Targeted water resource interventions (for example, watershed management in designated areas with poor farmers)
Interventions affecting water service delivery	*Type 3:* Broad water service delivery reforms (for example, reform of water supply utilities and water-user associations for irrigation management)	*Type 4:* Targeted water service reforms (for example, rural water supply and sanitation projects)

Source: World Bank 2003.

MANAGEMENT CHALLENGES

The main management challenge is not a vision of integrated water resource management but a principled (providing guidance on what needs to be done) and pragmatic (understanding that the art of reform is the art of the possible in specific circumstances) approach for improvement.

The Dublin Principles, forged for the 1992 Earth Summit, are widely accepted for sound water management. They state that water resources should be managed holistically and sustainably—ensuring participation and treating the resource as an economic good. Despite agreement on the principles, practice in the richest countries has improved only slowly—and it is still very far from ideal, especially for managing water as an economic good. The gap between principle and practice is wide in developing countries, especially for sound economic management of a scarce resource.

The new focus is on the basic economic principles. Sound water resource management requires that users take into account both the financial costs of supplying services and the costs that their use of water imposes on others ("opportunity costs").

Financial Costs

Pricing to cover financial costs is essential for two reasons. First, it provides the user with information on the cost of providing the service, thereby inducing more considerate use than if the service were free. Second, revenues from tariffs are the basis for maintaining existing and building new infrastructure.

Water and water services have traditionally been underpriced, resulting in inefficiency (and an inability to attract new investment) and inequity (because the poor inevitably are excluded). The political economy of pricing is quite different for services (such as urban water supply) that are local and not tradable and for services (such as irrigation water) that are inputs into products traded globally. Market structures are severely distorted, primarily by the more than US$300 billion a year in subsidies that rich countries provide to their agricultural producers.

In urban water supply, there is a clear movement toward broad application of the "user pays" principle, with positive results in efficiency, accountability, and the ability of utilities to serve the poor. In irrigation, too, there is movement toward modern forms of organization and financing, in which user payments become the centerpiece for transparent, accountable relations between providers and users. As distortions in global agricultural markets are reduced, the impetus for development of normal arrangements in irrigation services will increase.

Opportunity Costs

The use of water entails more than financial costs. When one person consumes water, other potential users may be denied the opportunity and value of such use. To ensure that water is allocated and used efficiently, countries must have institutional arrangements that ensure that these opportunity costs are taken into account. Here the central challenge is the development of a legal and enforceable system of water rights. Once established, such rights give rise to a series of fundamental and healthy changes:

- First, those that require additional resources (such as growing cities) will frequently be able to meet their needs by acquiring the rights of those that are using water for low-value purposes.
- Second, there are strong incentives for those that use water for low-value purposes to voluntarily give up their rights, making reallocation both politically attractive and practical.
- Third, establishing formal water rights gives rise to strong pressures to improve the data required to manage the resources.
- Fourth, establishing formal water rights reduces the pressures of a "race to the bottom," because those that have rights have a powerful interest in sustaining the resources.

There is no unanimity on the concept of water rights, for some see it as an unhealthy commodification of a public good. Nor is it simple to introduce rights-based systems for a fugitive resource in administratively weak environments with deep cultural implications. But there has been substantial progress in recent years (in Brazil, Chile, Mexico, and South Africa). And there are local pressures (villagers who store rainwater in Rajasthan, India) and international pressures (between Mexico and the United States) to define the rights to use an ever-scarcer resource.

Progress in implementing the Dublin Principles takes place one step at a time, heavily conditioned by broader political and economic realities. Needed is a reaffirmation of the Dublin Principles (ecological, institutional, and economic) and a shift in focus to implementation—to developing realistic, sequenced, and patient reform processes adapted to local realities.

Economic principles—such as ensuring that users take financial and resource costs into account when using water—are very important. And the solutions need to be tailored to specific, widely varying natural, cultural, economic, and political circumstances. The art of reform is in picking the low-hanging fruit first, not in making the best the enemy of the good. Architects of good reform recognize that the broader economic and fiscal and governance reforms often trigger reform opportunities in the water sector. They also recognize that reform processes are always political and, thus, that politicians who are willing to lead reform processes must be supported.

INVESTMENT IN INFRASTRUCTURE

Most developing countries have inadequate stocks of hydraulic infrastructure, such as dikes and dams, and face daunting financial challenges in developing such stocks. They need assistance in developing and maintaining appropriate stocks of well-performing infrastructure. The World Commission on Water estimates that annual investments in water infrastructure need to rise from US$75 billion today to US$180 billion by 2030. Attracting private investment will remain very important for many developing countries, but most financing of water infrastructure will continue to come from public sources.

The historical challenge of water resource management has been the reconciliation of human needs for predictable and regular flows of water with the variable patterns of precipitation and streamflow. The challenge is greatest where average flows are especially low and where variability is high.

Societies have long developed structural and nonstructural mechanisms for attempting this reconciliation, with two main lessons. First, infrastructure (dams, levies, and canals) is critical. Second, infrastructure investments need to be complemented by previously neglected nonstructural investments (in watershed management, land-use planning, and information and systems management). The emphasis in infrastructure-rich industrial countries is now heavily and appropriately focused on nonstructural solutions.

Major Challenges

First, many developing countries have stocks of water infrastructure that are a small fraction of those in climatically similar industrial countries (figure 5.1). Developing countries need to make large investments in infrastructure of all scales, ranging from local rainwater harvesting structures to major infrastructure such as dikes, canals, dams, and interbasin transfer schemes. Those investments need to follow good technical, economic, social, and environmental practices.

Second, they also have to invest simultaneously and heavily in nonstructural management solutions. Most developing countries have understood this need and are now doing so. Such efforts range from the massive efforts at watershed management in the Upper Yangtze

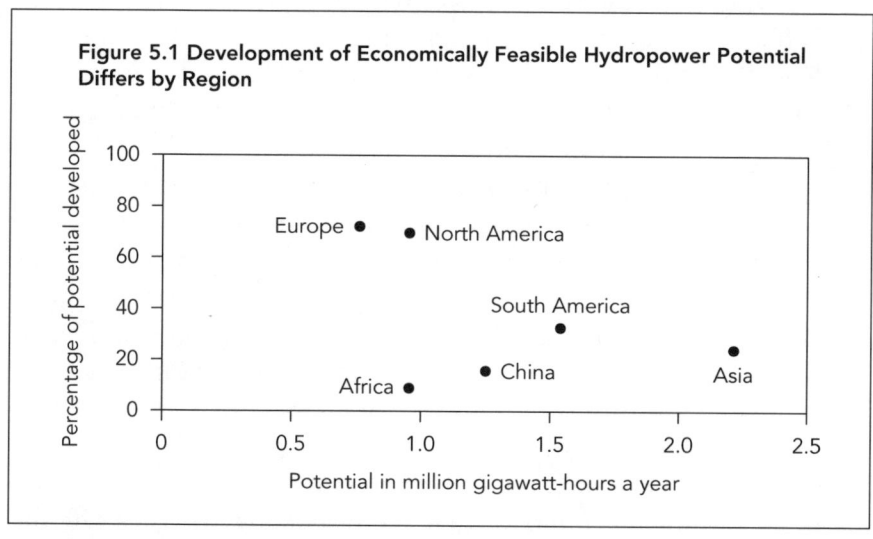

Figure 5.1 Development of Economically Feasible Hydropower Potential Differs by Region

Note: Data for Asia do not include China.
Source: World Bank 2003.

catchment in China to the development of improved hydrology data in India, to the elimination of water-using invasive alien plants in South Africa.

Third, global climate change accentuates the underlying imbalances between human demands and natural hydrological patterns, making the task of developing an integrated package of structural and nonstructural tools more urgent.

Major hydraulic infrastructure needs to be reconsidered, for four reasons:

- First, there have been improvements in recent decades in the way the social and environmental aspects of dams and other major water infrastructure have been addressed, and developing countries are committed to continuing improvement.
- Second, major water resource projects often form the basis for broad regional development, with significant direct and indirect benefits for the poor (and others). In India, for example, only 26 percent of people living in districts that have benefited from such projects are poor, in contrast to 69 percent in districts that have not so benefited.
- Third, as water scarcity in many countries becomes more acute, the costs of water infrastructure are rising rapidly. Many countries are having to invest in interbasin transfer schemes, with price tags of billions and even tens of billions of U.S. dollars. An analysis of World Bank "repeater" water supply projects shows that the cost of bulk water for the future project is often two to three times greater than that for the previous project.
- Fourth, among the governments of developing countries there is now a broad consensus that, although public funds have been and will remain indispensable, the required water infrastructure cannot be built with public funds alone. The private sector has an important complementary role. The Monterrey Conference on Development Financing highlights a need for the relevant international and regional institutions to increase their support for private foreign investment in infrastructure. Over the past decade, there has been a major change in the role of private financing of infrastructure in developing countries. Starting from a low base in 1990, the private sector has invested up to US$130 billion a year in infrastructure in developing countries to the year 2000.

A closer look shows that levels of private investment have declined dramatically in recent years. Furthermore, only a small proportion of private investment in infrastructure went into water-related infrastructure—about 5 percent into water and sanitation and another 5 percent into hydropower, concentrated in low-risk economies in East Asia and Latin America.

The Nile Basin

Since 1996, the Africa Water Resources Management Initiative has sought to improve national water resource management through institutional and legal review and reform, emphasizing ownership and stakeholder participation, environmental sustainability, demand management, and cost-efficiency. Often the point of entry for discussions of reform has been a client's request for major investments in infrastructure. Where the perceived investment needs are vast, a review of current practices and options is generally called for.

Africa has great needs for investments in water infrastructure. The share of the population with access to potable water is lower than that in any other region. The variability in rainfall is roughly three times that in temperate regions, but many African countries have per capita water storage (in reservoirs) in orders of magnitude less than industrial countries have. And countries have low levels of capacity to manage water resources as well as low levels of infrastructure investment, both of which must be addressed for either to be truly effective.

Complicating matters, Africa has more international rivers than any other continent. Tensions over the control of Nile waters are long-standing obstacles to growth and development in the region. Conflict prevention and cooperative water resource management are therefore central development challenges for the 10 countries sharing the Nile River.

The Nile Basin Initiative has a strategic action program guided by a shared vision to achieve sustainable socio-economic development through the equitable use of the Nile Basin water resources. The program includes a basinwide shared vision program of technical assistance projects designed to lay the foundation for cooperative action and two subbasin investment programs that will promote poverty reduction, economic growth, and better environmental management. Although the initiative's overarching goals are conflict prevention, poverty reduction, and environmental management—not simply the construction of major water infrastructure—the initiative's shared projects will deliver its most apparent and immediate development effects.

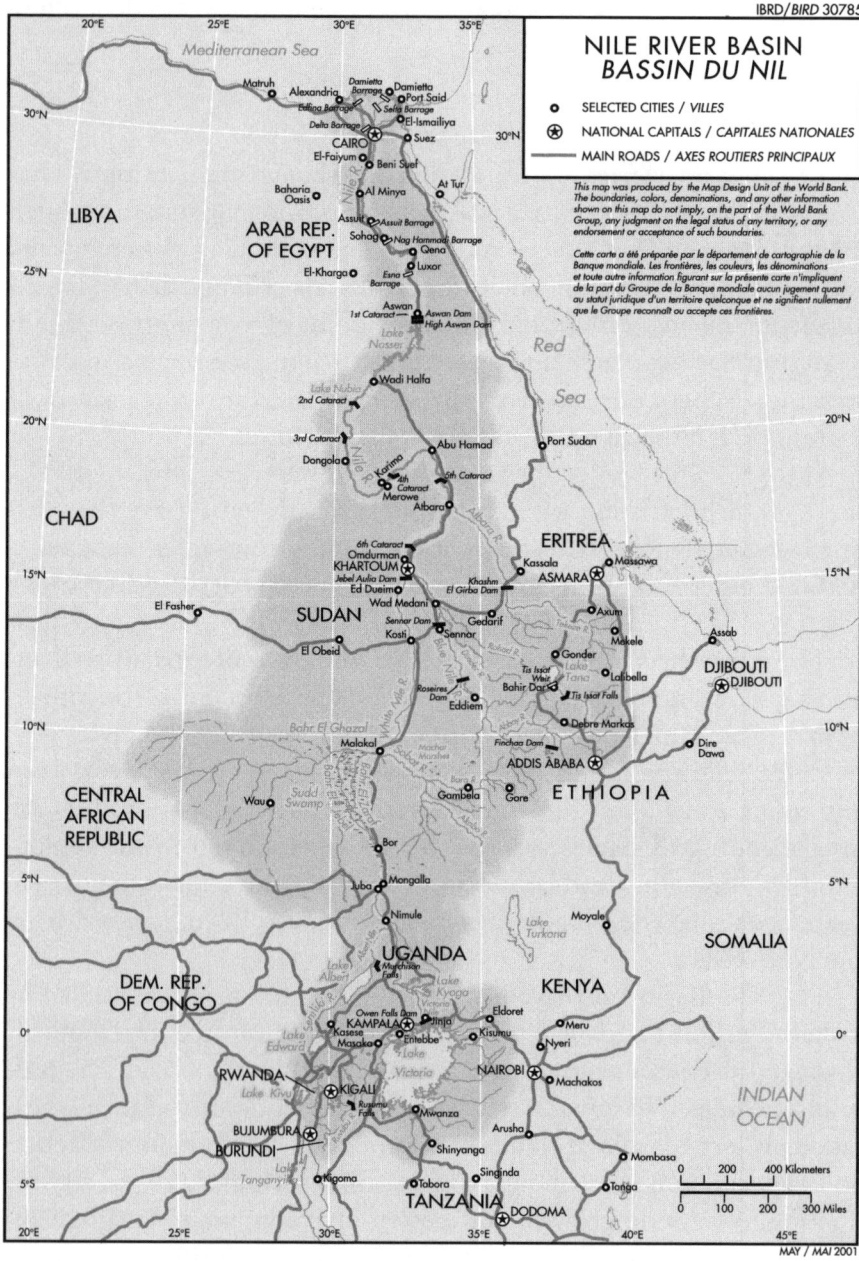

Map of the Nile River Basin.

The Nile Basin Initiative is led by the Council of Ministers of Water Affairs of the Nile Basin States and is supported by a small secretariat based in Entebbe, Uganda.

Some projects of the Nile Basin Initiative might find financing without significant donor involvement. But it is unlikely that all countries would be able to obtain funding, and the disparities in access to financing could increase tensions in the region. Moreover, the involvement of donor partners could increase the likelihood of best environmental and social practice.

Central Asia

The countries of Central Asia face water scarcity. Two rivers, the Amu Darya and Syr Darya, serve as the principal sources of water, especially for the downstream countries of Uzbekistan, Turkmenistan, and (southern) Kazakhstan, which have desert climates. Irrigation has been practiced in Central Asia for millennia, but the irrigated area almost doubled between 1950 and 1980, diverting large amounts of water from the rivers and reducing the water flow into the Aral Sea by about 80 percent.

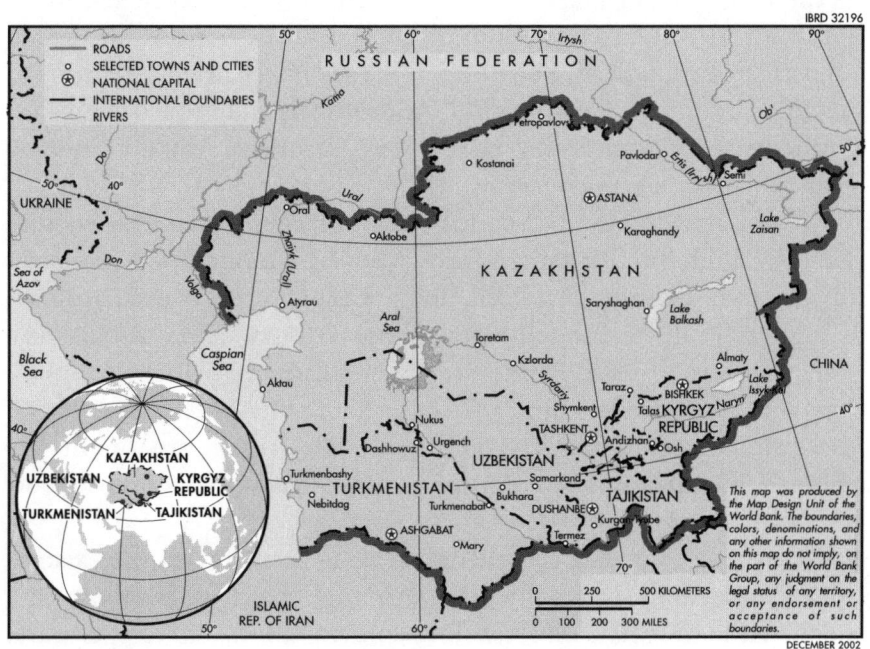

Map of Central Asia.

About 35 million people depend in one way or another on irrigated agriculture. But the effects of irrigation on the Aral Sea, whose surface area has declined by more than 50 percent over the past 40 years, have meant economic losses for the 3.5 million people living near the sea—from declining fisheries, loss of wetlands, and the health effects of blowing salt and highly saline shallow groundwater.

The countries of Central Asia face a unique set of challenges in developing and maintaining an appropriate stock of water infrastructure. For the most part, the problem is that there is more infrastructure than can be maintained. In irrigated areas, the World Bank has thus worked with borrowers in applying immediate "Band-aids" to critical infrastructure and also on developing medium-term strategies for "triage"—to determine which infrastructure (both supply and drainage) can and should be maintained and which abandoned.

Recent analysis suggests that rehabilitating infrastructure, along with managing demand, could reduce crop water requirements by more than 30 percent. It also shows that most serviced areas can be irrigated economically, even if users pay the operation and maintenance costs for water and drainage infrastructure. But water prices can be increased only when water delivery is reliable and when farmers can receive a fair market price for what they produce. Agriculture is now effectively taxed, with price and trade restrictions on several important commodities. So the key is to see water pricing reforms as part of a larger package of institutional reforms and infrastructure investments, with attention to sequencing, prioritization, and mechanisms for effecting transitions.

Urban water and sanitation utilities also face unique infrastructure challenges, inherited from the former Soviet Union. Domestic water supplies were heavily subsidized, and per capita use was extraordinarily high (typically about 400 liters per capita a day) and wasteful. As a result, both water supply and wastewater treatment plants were often overbuilt. As water use (and sewage production) has fallen to about 100 liters per capita a day, large overcapacity in treatment has emerged, and major pieces of infrastructure need to be mothballed or even abandoned.

For dams, the primary challenge is again to maintain the existing stock at a safe and serviceable level. Another challenge is monitoring and disseminating data on river flows, precipitation, and temperature.

With the decline in public funding in the past decade, hydrometeorological equipment has become outmoded and data systems are no longer reliable. Existing data series suggest that Central Asia will be affected by climate change, with temperatures, precipitation, and net evapotranspiration rising and extreme weather events becoming more frequent.

So the challenges of managing and developing water resources in Central Asia are daunting, and the solutions do not lie in the water sector alone. Instead, progress, as slow and difficult as it will be, will require concerted, integrated action across a wide range of areas—water-related sectors but also social sectors, governance, and macroeconomic and fiscal policy.

India: Andhra Pradesh

Investments in managing and developing water resources have done much to promote development, food security, and poverty reduction in India. They have led to an enormous increase in the production of food and food grains, benefiting the many poor people who are net food purchasers. They have helped reduce poverty, to the point that poverty rates in irrigated districts are only about a third of those in districts that are not irrigated. And they have had large multiplier effects in the economy.

In Andhra Pradesh, the challenge is to assist the state in its efforts to improve the management and development of its water resources. An emerging global software center, Andhra Pradesh has made good advances in collecting data but lags behind in interpreting and using those data for decisionmaking. The challenge includes developing a legal, regulatory, and institutional basis for making reallocation of water more flexible and voluntary. It thus calls for careful attention to the sensitive issue of users' water rights. It also means developing an approach to incorporating ecological requirements (for example, water releases into estuaries to sustain mangrove swamps and fisheries).

Those elements are key to an integrated river basin approach to water management, a central principle in the Indian National Water Policy and in the water policy of most Indian states. That approach fits well with the SMART (Simple Moral Accountable Responsive Transparent) philosophy of the government of Andhra Pradesh. But

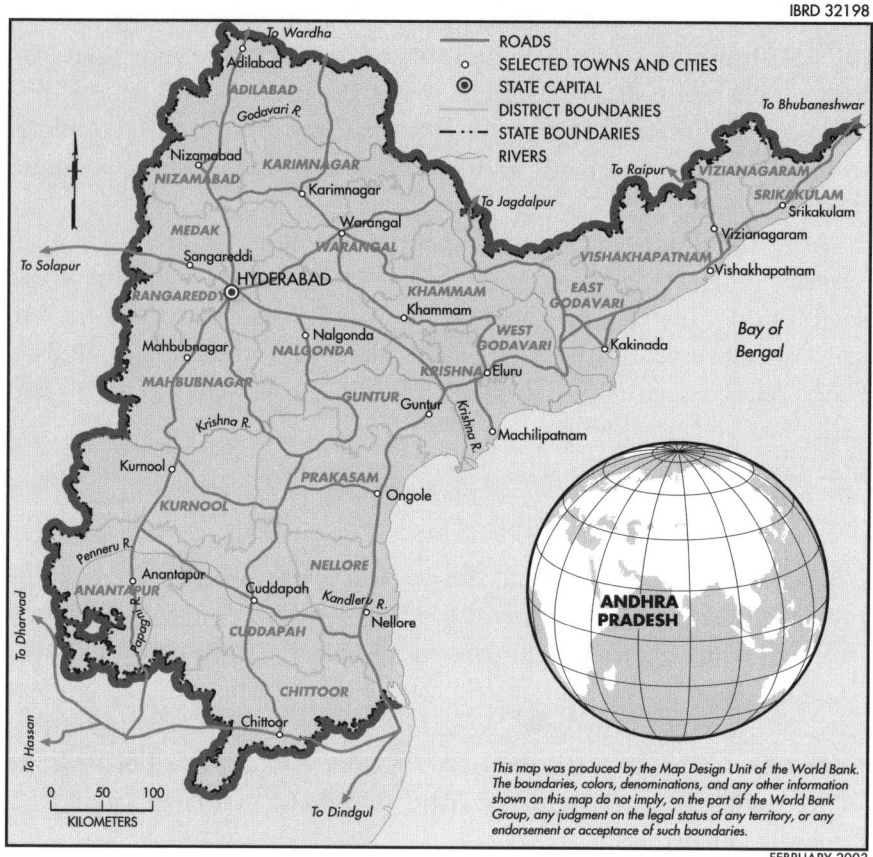

Map of Andhra Pradesh.

improving water resource management and development is a task that will take decades of persistence to complete, as well as a sequenced, prioritized program of actions tailored to the political realities as they evolve.

Many of the infrastructure challenges in India relate to the need to use existing infrastructure more effectively and to ensure the environmental and financial sustainability of that infrastructure. That said, challenges remain that relate to the development of new resources, as in Andhra Pradesh. The waters of one of the state's two major rivers (the Krishna) are fully developed, but the other major river (the Godavari) has lots of water. The problem is an elevation separation of about 300 meters from the place where the water is available to the place where there is land and a major demand for water (with entitlement issues going back to preindependence and with water scarcity contributing to security issues).

A simple economic analysis tells the state that developing those water resources for irrigation and hydropower is not the best use of limited financial resources. But the political and security imperatives are great. So although the state has decided not to build major dams (because of forest submersion and resettlement issues), it will probably proceed with some form of lift irrigation from the Godavari River.

A package of high-priority, well-justified (but not narrowly justified) investments would include modernization of major irrigation systems and some new investments, including possibly a phased, piloted lift scheme for the Godavari. Needed for that scheme is a strong emphasis on a carefully sequenced and prioritized program of institutional reforms, efficiency enhancements, and resource management measures both within the principal sectors (irrigation, water utilities) and for overall water resource management.

Andhra Pradesh shows that

- Water resource infrastructure can provide the basis for sustainable economic growth and poverty reduction and can even play an important part in improving relations among riparian countries.
- Water resource development must be accompanied by management reforms.
- Reforms are difficult and can be undertaken only when there is demonstrated local political leadership.
- When there is such leadership, the international community can bring new ideas to the table and invest in ways that make the reforms durable.
- Reforms are neither simple nor achieved in a day. The art of reform is defining a sequenced and prioritized set of reform actions and ensuring an appropriate incentive system for political leaders who take the risks inherent in reform.

CONCLUSIONS

The examples show that donor activities in water resources in any country should be the product of the water resource challenges in the country, the approach taken by the government, and the overall framework governing the relationship. Some broad themes are likely to play out in different contexts.

For water resource management, it is important to pay explicit attention to

- The wide variation in the underlying challenges—natural, economic, political, and social—and the wide variety of starting points. Those factors define the appropriate ambition and pace of reform.
- The need to move away from slogans based on principles and focus directly on issues of political economy. That means close attention to prioritizing and sequencing reform actions, taking advantage of windows of opportunity opened by economic and political reforms, understanding that the best should not become the enemy of the good, and operating with patience and persistence.
- The need to see water resource reforms through an expansive lens, going well beyond hydrology to the political, social, and cultural underpinnings.

For water infrastructure development, the following points are important:

- Most developing countries need to invest substantially in water infrastructure.
- The appropriate approach is not the old one of development first, management later, or the equally unbalanced management first, development later. What is required instead is a mix of investments in management *and* development.
- Donors must find more effective ways of becoming engaged if they are to have a seat at the table and serve as full-service advisory and investment partners to developing countries.

REFERENCES

World Bank. 2003. *Water Resources Sector Strategy: An Overview.* Washington, D.C.

———. 2004. "Water Resources Sector Strategy: Strategic Directions for World Bank engagement." Washington, D.C.

World Commission on Water. 2000. "A Water Secure World: Vision for Water, Life, and the Environment." Paris.

CHAPTER 6

WATER SUPPLY AND SANITATION FOR RESPONSIBLE GROWTH

S afe drinking water and adequate sanitation are central to improving the lives of the poor, yet an estimated 1.1 billion people lack access to safe water, 2.4 billion are without adequate sanitation, and more than 4 billion do not have their wastewater treated to any degree. In the developing world, about 2 of every 10 people lack access to safe water supply (1.5 billion), 5 of every 10 lack adequate sanitation (2.5 billion), and 9 of every 10 do not have their wastewater treated to any degree (4.5 billion). The levels of access vary between regions and between urban and rural areas. Population growth will increase these numbers dramatically. For example, the urban population is expected to grow by more than 1 billion people in the coming 15 years, 2 billion in the next 30, and 3 billion in the next 50. Much of that growth will be in the numerous—and harder to reach—secondary cities and towns.

If the Millennium Development Targets for water supply and sanitation are to be met, about 300,000 people a day will have to be provided with sustainable access to safe water, and almost 400,000 a day will require basic sanitation (figure 6.1). The greatest needs are in East Asia and the Pacific, South Asia, and Sub-Saharan Africa (figure 6.2). For this accomplishment to occur, investments in water supply and sanitation will need to double from past values of about

This chapter builds on the World Bank's Water and Sanitation Strategy (World Bank 2004) and is a collaborative effort, with contributions by Jamal Saghir and Meike Van Ginneken of the Energy and Water Department.

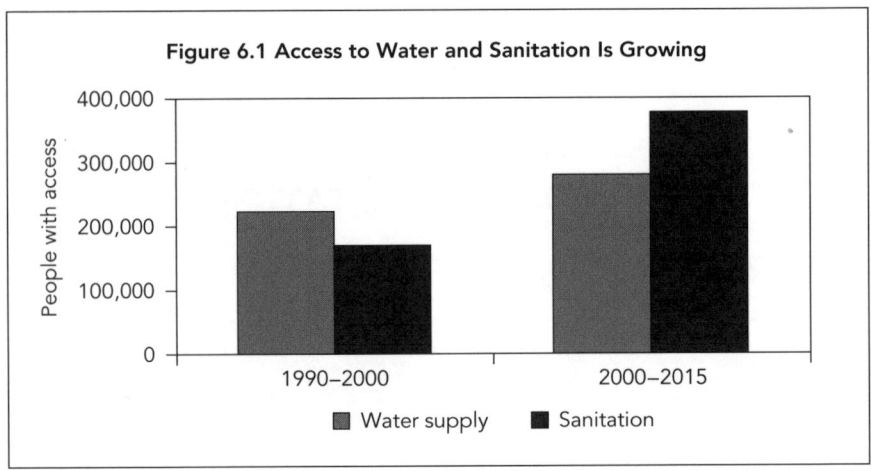

Figure 6.1 Access to Water and Sanitation Is Growing

Note: Number of new people with access to water supply and sanitation per day for past 10 years and projection for 2000–2015.
Source: UNICEF 2004.

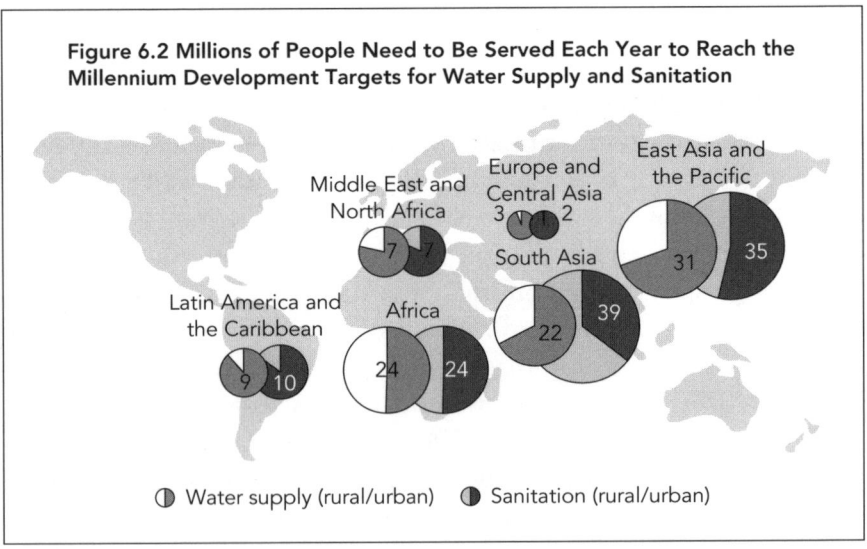

Figure 6.2 Millions of People Need to Be Served Each Year to Reach the Millennium Development Targets for Water Supply and Sanitation

Source: UNICEF 2004.

US$15 billion a year to reach US$30 billion. The US$30 billion annual estimate assumes, however, higher investment and operating efficiency than most countries have realized so far. Those global estimates exclude the much larger potential demand for treating collected wastewater and disposing of it in an environmentally sustainable fashion. Even simple treatment systems add significantly to the overall cost of providing water supply and sanitation services, although they are often necessary for environmental and health-related reasons.

The estimates are also based on proximity to a physical installation, rather than on the quality or reliability of the water supply and sanitation services that are available, and thus tend to exaggerate access levels. Counting technological improvements has routinely been used as an indicator for water supply. In reality, effective local water supply and sanitation service delivery are the result of a chain of social, political, economic, technical, and environmental decisions and conditions, and the outcome is contingent on the strength of each link. Sustainable access to water supply and sanitation requires not only technology but also a system of governance to support the operation and maintenance of that technology over time.

Improving access to water supply and sanitation services is an essential part of poverty reduction. It is critical to progress in health, education, gender equality, and environmental sustainability. Water supply and sanitation services generate a wide range of direct and indirect benefits for individuals and communities. For example, providing latrines in schools increases primary school enrollment. Improving access to safe water sources frees women from spending hours each day collecting water. And achieving higher education levels for mothers reduces the incidence of water-related diseases in children. Over the long term, the socio-economic costs of poor water supply and sanitation are much more expensive and disruptive than the cost of ensuring that the poor have access to these vital services.

The provision of water supply and sanitation services is at the heart of building sustainable communities in which people can take control of their lives and make real strides on the path to development. Even rudimentary water supply and sanitation services provide dignity to people and improve their health. Given the many socio-economic benefits of water supply and sanitation services, the development community recognizes that their effective provision is a vital element of responsible policies that seek to ensure sustained increases in human welfare.

WATER SUPPLY AND SANITATION IS A MILLENNIUM PRIORITY

The Millennium Summit, the Conference on Finance for Development at Monterrey, and the World Summit on Sustainable Development at Johannesburg moved water supply and sanitation out of its narrow sectoral purview and placed it firmly at the center of the broader poverty reduction agenda.

At the Millennium Summit in 2000, world leaders adopted the Millennium Development Goals—to sustain development and eliminate poverty. The goals are an interconnected framework of goals and targets that provide yardsticks for measuring global progress in achieving significant improvements in people's lives. Under the goal of ensuring environmental sustainability, two Millennium Development Targets are for water supply and sanitation:

- To reduce by half, by 2015, the proportion of people who lack sustainable access to safe drinking water
- To reduce by half, by 2015, the proportion of people who lack access to basic sanitation

Other targets, such as reducing the mortality rate of children under 5 years of age by two-thirds, are implicitly related to improving sustainable access to water supply and sanitation services. In South America, for example, it has been estimated that increasing water supply and sanitation coverage to 100 percent would reduce under-5 mortality that is due to waterborne diseases by 22 percent.

The Millennium Development Goals are laudable, but it is important to keep in mind that reaching them gets us only part of the way to serving the world's 9 billion people in 2050. Between now and then, infrastructure investments in developing countries will need to rise from US$200 billion a year to nearly US$1.5 trillion a year, a good part of that for water supply and sanitation.

Millennium Development Targets in water supply and sanitation should not be interpreted as a binary system of access and lack of access, which would require only connecting the unserved in order to be met. Emphasis has to be placed on providing sustainable access to those services. Thus, actions to improve existing services and to connect the unserved are both urgently needed. The challenge of the goals is to ensure a continuous process of improvement—strengthening informal service providers, upgrading aged facilities, and securing the long-term financial and institutional capacity necessary to restore, operate, maintain, and expand water supply and sanitation infrastructure.

At Monterrey, more than 100 heads of government pledged themselves to a new global compact. Developing countries agreed to implement sound policies, strengthen governance systems, and invest in their people. Rich countries agreed to increase their international assistance and take action on trade. At the Johannesburg Summit, it was agreed that progress in water and sanitation was one of the five key areas needed to improve the lives of all human beings while preserving the environment. The sanitation target was one of the few new international commitments at the World Summit on Sustainable Development, thus reflecting its centrality in improving human welfare.

Those key agreements challenge all actors to translate internationally recognized priorities into improvements on the ground. Only by dispensing with ideological debates in the water supply and sanitation sector and through the concerted action of all actors—communities, governments, the private sector, nongovernmental organizations, international organizations, and academia—can improvements be made. The enormous challenges can be met only if the energy and commitment of all those actors is harnessed to promote the cost-effective use of water resources and to mobilize resources to support water supply and sanitation activities.

INVESTMENT WITHOUT REFORM WILL NOT REACH THE GOALS

The magnitude of the water supply and sanitation challenge put forth by the international community and embodied in the Millennium Development Goals requires that limited resources be used to full advantage. Acting on lessons learned from experience, including those of the International Drinking Water and Sanitation Decade, is necessary to ensure that the investments do not gloss over complex problems or lead to unsustainable solutions. Higher levels of investment are necessary to reach the Millennium Development Goals, but alone such investment will not be sufficient to sustain service and expand access.

One of the most important lessons from decades of experience in providing water supply and sanitation services to the poor is that investments in infrastructure without concomitant policy and institutional reforms are ultimately ineffectual. Reforms to change the incentives in the sector are the first priority. Appropriate incentives can increase financial flows, achieve better returns on investment, improve the performance of service providers, and modify public and industrial demand for water. Reforms that support accountable, efficient, equitable, and effective service providers are needed to supply water and sanitation services over the long term. Creating and sustaining them often requires hard political decisions and changes to existing policies. So in any given city, town, or village, the real challenge of providing water supply and sanitation services to the poor quickly leaves the technical realm and enters the political. In many ways, the problem is best understood as a governance issue.

Given the complex multidisciplinary nature of water issues in all countries, building professional capacity to run institutions creates the foundation for introducing and sustaining new sector approaches. Policies, institutions, and financial arrangements are only as good as the people who implement them. Developing in-country capacity in a full range of technical, managerial, and operational disciplines is necessary if the sector is to be transformed.

Related to governance and capacity is the lesson that overall control of the policy environment and the resource must remain the responsibility of sovereign governments. But their roles should change. Using private or local community agencies to deliver services is an effective way to improve performance. Ensuring efficient, affordable, and sustainable access to safe water supply and sanitation requires engagement with efficient service providers along the entire spectrum of public and private involvement.

PEOPLE ARE AT THE CENTER OF SUSTAINABLE WATER SUPPLY AND SANITATION

Experience has shown that communities can make responsible decisions about investments in sustainable water supply and sanitation and will pay for them if they are made responsible and accountable for managing the systems. Few countries have implemented broad reforms that put people at the center.

Bringing in diverse views will improve the outcome of reform. Many groups have an interest in the delivery of safe and sustainable water, but not all objectives may coincide. Those that govern the sector may be concerned with overall performance. Individual households may be mainly interested in the quality, reliability, and costs of the service. Labor unions, environmental advocates, service providers, and other interest groups may all have views on how reform should be implemented. Thus, it is essential to use consultative processes that are genuinely inclusive, transparent, and well informed.

DELIVERING SAFE WATER AND SANITATION COSTS MONEY

The issue of paying for water supply and sanitation services presents an important, yet counterintuitive, lesson: the poor now pay more money for inferior services. Many poor households purchase their water from local water vendors at a cost 4 to 100 times that of water from a piped supply. This water is at risk of being contaminated either at its source or during its collection and transportation. Large public subsidies often fail to reach poor households, either because these households are not connected to formal services or because they are forced to use substandard public or private facilities.

Enshrining water as a universal human right that should be provided free is persuasive rhetoric. But it is also a risky distraction that stands in the way of providing water for all. Building, maintaining, and operating infrastructure to get water to households—pipes, treatment works, and connections—cost money. There are only two sources for investment: payments by users and payments by taxpayers. Only by charging those who are served can services be extended to the unconnected. Tariff setting must include subsidies to the poor. But advocating free water for all means no water for many.

More investment is needed to reach the Millennium Development Goals, but it is equally important to obtain greater productivity from existing investments through policies that promote efficiency and create local and national capacity. Indeed, where networks are already developed, more efficient and sustainable operation of existing infrastructure deserves priority over capital investment.

Pricing of water and water services is often a contentious issue. In general, the income derived from the tariff is the basis for building and maintaining existing infrastructure, and pricing provides the user with information on the value of the resource or service, hence inducing more considerate use than if it were free. Water and water services have traditionally been underpriced, thereby resulting in inefficient use by households and industries that have access to cheap water. Underpricing has also left the water sector with too few financial resources to be self-financing.

More investment in the water supply and sanitation sector must go hand in hand with the recognition that water pricing is an essential instrument to enhance the financing sustainability of the operation, maintenance, and expansion of services. The only way to reach the Millennium Development Goals is to charge those who can pay and to subsidize those who cannot. Generating cash flows through cost recovery is essential for all service providers, but tariff adjustment can often be implemented only gradually.

SANITATION AND HYGIENE REQUIRE SPECIAL ATTENTION

The unique characteristics of sanitation and hygiene require different approaches to service provision. Sanitation and hygiene are more than simple add-ons to water supply. For example, the order of introducing sanitation infrastructure, starting with household facilities and followed by public infrastructure, differs from the order of introducing water supply. Stepwise approaches may be necessary to meet the short- and long-term needs of the community. Meeting changing community needs over time requires more emphasis on rooting sanitation more firmly in the urban development agenda—in city planning, slum upgrading, security of tenure, building codes and bylaws, housing development, and microcredit.

Demand for sanitation and the willingness to pay for sanitation services generally lag behind demand for water. Spending money on infrastructure without investing in social marketing and support will not achieve the desired health or environmental gains. Why? Because behavioral change is essential to achieving those gains. Ultimately, the benefits of improved sanitation and hygiene depend largely on decisions made at the household level. So sanitation and hygiene programs require long-term commitments—not just investment.

The lack of sanitation and hygiene affects everyone. Changes in sanitation and hygiene are essential to improve health and reduce poverty. Away from the home, the provision of sanitation services (wastewater collection and treatment, drainage, and so on) yields significant benefits to society. But individually water supply, sanitation, and good hygiene are not sufficient to eliminate illness caused by waterborne disease—they are all required.

Given the importance of social and cultural mores related to sanitation and health issues, a single management model will not be sufficient to deliver universal sanitation services. Traditional supply-driven approaches—with services planned and provided by professionals without reference to consumer preferences and the willingness to pay—have often proven unsustainable. Innovative ways of providing access to sanitation and hygiene need to be developed, piloted, and scaled up wherever possible. Such ways include promoting public-private partnerships and improving access to information.

SAFE WATER SUPPLY REQUIRES WORKING WITH OTHERS

Reforms in water supply and sanitation are strongly political, requiring sequenced, practical, and patient interventions. Multiple interests must be balanced. Tradeoffs have to be made, in which there may be short-term losers, especially among those with vested interests in the status quo.

Improving water supply and sanitation services requires working through other sectors. Water supply and sanitation sector priorities can be achieved only if they are integrated into the government's strategic objectives (including health, education, and land-use objectives) and resources are allocated accordingly. And water users must cooperate. Water is essential not only for drinking but also for food production, industry, hydropower, and other uses. The use of water resources for building livelihoods must not compromise the sustainability of vital ecosystems. Allocation of water between competing uses calls for integrated water resource management and infrastructure development that transcends compartmentalized sector concerns. The deterioration of water quality upstream reduces the usability of the resource for downstream water supply. Municipal wastewater hampers others downstream. The poor suffer most if realistic water pollution policies are not set and enforced.

A RESPONSE TO THE INTERNATIONAL CHALLENGE IS NEEDED

National and local governments around the world are struggling to provide their citizens with sustainable and affordable access to water supply and sanitation services. Each set of local political, environmental, cultural, and socio-economic conditions requires its own unique solution. Countries need to set and implement priorities and strategies that support local aspirations and fully use the resources available. Those strategies should include policies to close gaps in access and financing and to build the institutional capacity to execute and scale up service delivery. Experience shows that countries can move toward sustainable access to water supply and sanitation services for all with a four-pronged response to the challenge:

1. *Policies.* Adopting policies that provide incentives to invest and operate efficiently and provide sustainable services that reach the poor.
2. *Institutions.* Building and strengthening local institutions to scale up activities.
3. *Knowledge.* Creating and disseminating knowledge necessary at all levels—policymakers, managers, staff, and consumers—for setting priorities and using resources to maximum advantage.
4. *Financing.* Securing the necessary financing to rebuild infrastructure and expand service coverage and quality.

Policies to Expand Access and Sustain Service

Investments in water supply and sanitation must be supported by a sound policy framework. The long-term operation and maintenance of water supply and sanitation infrastructure requires the political stability that clearly defined rules and regulations provide. Policies that support and encourage the efficient and effective operation, maintenance, and expansion of existing infrastructure can have a dramatic effect on the ability of a local service provider to extend services to the poor.

Providing Clear Accountability and Incentives. Accountability for performance requires a clear separation of functions and responsibilities, with policymakers specifying the goals and standards. The specification of goals and standards permits the evaluation of actual service delivery. But public service providers rarely operate under specific targets—nor are sanctions imposed if they fail to meet such targets.

Many utilities operate with unaccounted water in excess of 50 percent and with payment collections below 70 percent. So only about one-third of the water produced generates revenue. Utilities need incentives to convert these "lost" cubic meters into cubic meters consumed, billed, and collected. China shows how an incentive program based on clearly delineated roles and responsibilities can provide the foundation for a successful and accountable water supply and sanitation program (box 6.1).

Serving the Poor. Water supply and sanitation policies must shift from building new infrastructure to maintaining and using existing capacity to meet consumer demand. Service providers are capable of tailoring their supply to the preferences and incomes of the unserved

---

Box 6.1   China's Rural Water Program: Connecting Improved Service to Sustainable Financing

About 6 million households have benefited from improved services under China's rural water supply and sanitation program. Central government loans finance 50 percent of the capital cost, whereas provincial and county governments jointly finance 25 percent. Grants and users contribute a full 25 percent, usually as a combination of cash and labor. Users pay operating costs and debt service, effectively raising their overall contribution to 75 percent.

Households are metered, and a strong incentive system ties the salaries of operations staff members to monthly collections. Payment compliance is usually more than 90 percent, and nonpayment is rare. When tariffs do not cover operating costs, they are raised. The key to success is the government's willingness to price—and enforce—rural water supply services at financially sustainable levels. In addition, households that have individual piped water connections pay more than households that receive lower levels of service. The county price bureaus act as watchdogs to protect the interests of consumers, the rural poor, and providers.

poor, although doing so often requires special programs and approaches to stimulate demand and address the service preferences and means of payment of the poor. In many cases, not much additional production is needed: studies on all continents indicate that low-income consumers manage well with 30 to 50 liters per capita per day and that consumption by the poorest 20 percent of the population typically accounts for about 6 percent of a city's total water consumption. This additional consumption can often be met by increasing operating efficiency: in almost all cities, levels of leakage and unaccounted water are unacceptably high.

Demand-driven design permits the adaptation of service standards and costs to income levels and household preferences. It also allows for the gradual upgrade of service standards in line with the growth of household income and demand. To this end, some utilities in urban areas are mapping the unserved populace and providing water supply through steadily denser supply points and, eventually, house connections. This staged approach satisfies demand at the least cost and makes service affordable. Utilities must concentrate greater efforts and resources on programs targeting the unserved. In areas on the urban periphery, a first step toward staged and demand-driven design might include supplying bulk water to small entrepreneurs who distribute it to low-income people at affordable rates.

Institutional Capacity to Improve Service Delivery

Building and strengthening institutional capacity to deliver water supply and sanitation services is an urgent and ongoing task. Providing water supply and sanitation service is a complex, multidisciplinary field. Managerial and technical capacity is needed not only in large cities but also in the millions of smaller cities, towns, and villages throughout the world. Strong institutions are better able to generate cash flows, close revenue cycles, and attract additional financing or investment. Creating the conditions to motivate people to take on responsibility for providing efficient and effective service is a precondition for sustainable delivery.

Providing Specific Solutions for Rural Services. Experience has shown that rural water supply and sanitation programs work best when they are demand driven. Community management is fundamental to sustainability. The ingredients for successful rural water supply and sanitation systems include the following:

- *Demand responsiveness*, which implies that the community initiates and helps plan, implement, maintain, and then own the systems.
- *Women*, who play a key role since they stand the most to gain if the systems are successful.
- *Private providers* of goods and services, who can speed project implementation and introduce clear accountability for the quality of equipment and workmanship, possibly under performance-based arrangements.

What does it take to motivate communities to take on the responsibility for keeping costs down and keeping the system running? Systems have to be designed with community input to meet the community's particular needs. The community has to manage the execution of the works. The community has to contribute to the capital costs. And the community has to be given ownership rights to the assets (box 6.2).

Box 6.2 Community-Based Water Supply and Sanitation Project in Uttar Pradesh, India

The rural water and sanitation project known as Swajal takes a community-based, demand-responsive approach. The project has established full cost recovery for operation and maintenance and partial cost recovery for capital costs—both major departures from past practice in the Indian water sector. Implementation of water supply, sanitation, and such community empowerment activities as health awareness, women's development, and informal education are undertaken by a partnership of village committees, nongovernmental organizations, and a project management unit.

Giving user communities control over financial resources is a key feature of community-driven development. Swajal was one of the first major rural water and sanitation projects to shift from centralized procurement and transfer investment funds to user communities, enabling these communities to procure materials, services, and works by themselves, assisted by support organizations. Support organizations include nongovernmental organizations, which assist with community mobilization, establishment of village water and sanitation committees, and development of design choices, and private firms, which provide technical design, inspection, and monitoring services.

Recent appraisals of sustainability have shown that up to 97 percent of schemes are fully functional and that there is a high rate of latrine use in villages that participated in the project. The Swajal project is now being used as a model by the Indian government in its National Water Sector Reform Program.

Expanding Private-Public Partnerships. There is an urgent need to move beyond the stale and polarized debate on public or private involvement in the sector. The debate should not be about public or private service delivery—it should be about sustainable access to safe water supply and sanitation services at the lowest cost. The World Bank's overarching premise for the water supply and sanitation sector centers on ensuring efficient, affordable, and sustainable access to safe water supply and sanitation. That means engaging with efficient service providers along the spectrum of public and private involvement. Improvements can be made only through concerted action on the part of all parties.

Public-private partnerships grew rapidly in the 1990s in most developing regions, as governments sought private financing to substitute for scarce public funding and sought private management to improve service efficiency and quality. The number of large public-private partnerships in water supply and sanitation grew from a handful in the 1980s to approximately 200 in 1990–2001. Those arrangements are estimated to serve an aggregate population in excess of 250 million people. This figure does not include either the many local tenders issued by medium-size cities or the multitude of small providers working with and through local governments, village water committees, and utilities.

It is clear that those partnerships are not a panacea for resolving all of the sector's performance shortcomings. The success of public-private partnerships in bringing sustained benefits to consumers rests on appropriately allocating and managing the risks and responsibilities between the government and the private sector. A partnership means that risks and rewards are shared. Only the public partner—government—can manage political risk, including setting clear rules for adjusting tariffs. Moreover, currency risk is considerable when investment programs are financed by external nonconcessional borrowings. But the private partner must fully bear the performance risks (construction, operational, commercial) if taxpayers and consumers are to benefit from the partnership.

Regulation and oversight should be grounded in regulating by results rather than in micromanaging inputs. Well-structured public-private partnerships require goals and performance targets that are clearly defined and accountability that is explicit in the contractual arrangements. This structure in turn allows for public scrutiny and promotes a culture of public accountability. The success of public-private partnership in Senegal shows the benefits from this mode of service provision (box 6.3).

Box 6.3   Public-Private Partnership in Senegal

Senegal has made remarkable progress in bringing water and sanitation services to low-income areas in Dakar and in secondary cities. A private operator improved service through investment and through applying modern management and know-how. It became possible to balance the cash flow for the first time in decades, thus permitting the utility to get commercial financing for a major investment.

A second phase of the program focused on further institutional and regulatory reform under the performance-based contract. It increased water production and distribution capacities and rehabilitated sewerage networks. It also implemented demand-driven community-based programs for onsite and neighborhood sanitation services and technical assistance to strengthen the capacities of sector agencies and communities.

The program was connecting about 60,000 low-income households under a comprehensive program of public standpipes and economical house connections. Unaccounted water decreased from 31 percent in 1996 to 22 percent in 2001, and the private operator improved the quality of water supplied.

Knowledge to Inform Governments, Empower Consumers, and Challenge Operators

The design and implementation of improved water supply and sanitation policies and the strengthening of water supply and sanitation institutions are both supported by improved knowledge of the sector and its relationship to other sectors, such as energy and land use. Knowledge can be obtained through access to information, education, and training opportunities. Transparency is an important part of effective knowledge transfer. It can empower consumers, operators, and governments by allowing them to compare and contrast the performance of utilities both against their past performance and against the performance of other similar utilities:

- Consumers are better able to make the political case for more effective water supply and sanitation services when they have a thorough understanding of their local service delivery mechanisms.

- Operators can make the case for improved budget allocations and enhanced political support for their services when they can clearly demonstrate the links between those activities and the success of their operations.
- Governments benefit from a more informed electorate and a more organized utility through enhanced public understanding of the need for investment and change.

Strengthening Local Authorities. In many areas, local authorities are responsible for providing water supply and sanitation services. To make informed decisions, they need access to meaningful and targeted information on the importance of setting practical goals, making alternative service delivery arrangements, and using outsourcing methods. They also need information on service quality and efficiency if they are to begin to hold their service providers accountable.

Knowledge sharing among local governments on tangible and practical ways to improve the quality of water supply and sanitation services is more effective than knowledge transfers from international consultants. Benchmarking performance and public disclosure permits municipalities and consumers to compare the service they receive against service in other towns and cities. In particular, they can determine whether they are paying for inefficiencies or poor service. Comparative regulation will also bring benefits over time as consumers and governments become better informed. In the meantime, "regulation by sunshine," which emphasizes transparency in the details of service provision, can provide local operators with some modest incentive to improve service access and quality.

Providing Professional Services. Developing local technical, managerial, and operational capacity requires an enormous effort. In recognition of the local nature of water supply and sanitation service delivery, traditional formal training programs for national cadres of civil servants have given way to programs that build on the existing expertise of local entrepreneurs, commercial establishments, and community and civic groups. Programs to develop small and medium-size enterprises, local capacity enhancement through nongovernmental organizations, and microcredit facilities are benefiting local utilities. Ongoing technical and operational support systems are needed to provide specialized professional support to local operators, whether public or private, on an as-needed basis. Such systems are especially crucial to smaller operators in small cities and towns, which have limited in-house resources.

Empowering Consumers. Efforts to strengthen the capacity of local water operators must be matched by efforts to empower consumers. Consumers need information about a diverse range of issues: how to draw and consume water safely, how to dispose of excreta safely, how to convey good hygiene habits to families, and how to ensure the quality of local water supplies. Consumers also need public information that evaluates local utilities' performance against clearly elaborated goals and standards. Thus armed, they can hold public officials, as well as public and private service providers, accountable for their policies, actions, and uses of funds.

Hygiene and sanitation promotion programs have had a very mixed record in this aspect. Those successful in stimulating demand and behavioral change have focused on what households and communities want and are motivated to invest in. They have identified core messages—for example, sanitation as a consumer good, rather than as a health benefit—and targeted clients whose behaviors or spending decisions are most critical (often mothers and children). They have also aggressively marketed the product. Box 6.4 provides an example

---

Box 6.4   Knowledge and Intersectoral Collaboration Can Make a Difference

In the 1990s, four private soap companies launched hand-washing campaigns in Costa Rica, El Salvador, and Guatemala in collaboration with the public sector. Behavioral research determining hand-washing habits were the basis for communication programs and community activities. The documented results included a 30 percent increase in correct hand-washing behavior by mothers and 320,000 fewer cases of diarrhea per year in poor children under 5 years old in Guatemala.

The World Bank, the London School of Hygiene and Tropical Medicine, and private soap companies—in collaboration with the U.S. Agency for International Development, the United Nations Children's Fund, and the Centers for Disease Control and Prevention—are implementing a global initiative to promote hand washing with soap in developing countries. Public-private partnerships have been established in China, Ghana, Nepal, Peru, and Senegal.

of how consumer empowerment can prevent health problems associated with poor hygiene.

Secure Financing to Rebuild Infrastructure, Expand Service Coverage, and Improve Quality

Expanding access to water supply requires money. Increasing investments will depend on the ability of service providers to generate more cash flow from operations. Public, private, and international financing sources need to be combined to support the long-term investments and running costs of water service provision. Governments are responsible for about three-quarters of financing in the water supply and sanitation sector and, in the years to come, will remain responsible for the majority of investments. The private sector and external support agencies each previously accounted for approximately 10 percent of water supply and sanitation financing in developing countries, though those amounts have fallen in recent years. Household investments and other sources cover the remainder. To the greatest extent possible, this financial support must come from local and national sources—financing denominated in foreign currencies is more expensive. However, raising private investment financing locally is constrained by weak local financial markets in many developing countries.

Sustainable Financial Policies. Expanding and sustaining water supply and sanitation services require clear and consistent financial policies. The extent and manner of cost recovery are central. Policymakers essentially face three choices:

- User charges that depend on the level of costs, the demand for services, and the level of consumer income.
- Generalized subsidies financed by taxpayers.
- Deferral of the expenses necessary for sustaining service.

The choices have far-reaching economic consequences. Willingness to charge for services is as much an issue as willingness to pay. Reliance on user charges to recover costs offers the best prospects for aligning service with demand when the operator's remuneration is tied to its revenues. Generalized subsidies financed by tax receipts carry the risk of supply-driven investments and may dilute provider accountability to consumers. Cutting expenditures (rather than costs) perpetuates unsatisfactory service and ultimately widens the access gap. The consequences are deteriorating infrastructure and higher costs to consumers.

Willingness to Pay. The financing of sanitation and wastewater investments presents particular challenges because costs cannot be easily recovered from users—least of all from low-income households. Yet the economic returns from providing the services are high. To keep subsidies at reasonable levels, experience across regions indicates that community involvement in all phases helps ensure service levels in line with what people actually want to use and to which they are prepared to contribute. Consumer willingness to pay is greater for wastewater collection and for sanitary excreta disposal because those services represent a tangible improvement of living conditions. But the costs of conveyance and treatment are more difficult to recover because consumers do not readily perceive the benefits of such investments, which are much more costly.

CONCLUSIONS

The challenge set forth by the international community for increased sustainable access to water supply and sanitation services is one that can be met only through the concerted effort of a wide variety of actors. From individual decisions to local priorities, national plans, and international assistance, engaging people in the development of sustainable solutions is of utmost priority. The needs of poor communities to live with dignity and to realize their potential, along with the significant benefits for society and the environment that can be realized through improved water supply and sanitation programs, are too great to be shunted aside in favor of quick fixes and unsustainable investments. Meeting internationally accepted goals in water supply and sanitation will occur only if investment decisions are accepted and supported by the communities they are meant to serve, if national priorities are clearly defined, and if institutions are empowered to take on the task of supporting and maintaining water supply and sanitation systems through sound policy frameworks, sustainable financial frameworks, and increased national and local capacity.

REFERENCES

UNICEF (United Nations Children's Fund). 2004. "UNICEF Statistics: Water and Sanitation." Available at http://www.childinfo.org/eddb/water.htm.

World Bank. 2004. "The World Bank Group's Program for Water Supply and Sanitation." Washington, D.C.

CHAPTER 7

THE ENVIRONMENT AS A RESOURCE FOR DEVELOPMENT

The economic costs of environmental degradation have been estimated at 4 to 8 percent of gross domestic product (GDP) annually in many developing countries. Why such high costs? A variety of reasons: distorted policies, governance structures, institutional frameworks, incentives, and pressures to export natural resources without investments in human or infrastructure capital tend to favor a short-term focus that follows a "grow now, clean up later" approach to development.

The challenge for the development community is to work with developing countries to design and implement policies, programs, and investments that are based on good analysis and the participation of key stakeholders. The policies, programs, and investments must not only support continued economic development, but also focus on reducing poverty, avoid sacrificing the interest of future generations, and build on the emerging global consensus that natural resources and other valuable environmental assets must be managed sustainably as countries follow a path of responsible growth.

Improving environmental policies and mitigating the environmental impacts of sectoral policies are an integral element of the agenda for achieving the Millennium Development Goals. Goal 7—to ensure environmental sustainability—aims to mainstream the environment in policy and programs, reverse the loss of environmental resources, and improve access to environment-related services. The

This chapter builds on the World Bank's Environment Strategy (World Bank 2001) and was prepared by Warren Evans, Todd Johnson, and Ede Jorge Ijjasz-Vasquez of the Environment Department.

importance of the environment is reinforced by its strong linkages to the rest of the goals. It is difficult to imagine being able to reduce income-poverty in rural areas where land is degraded. Reductions in child mortality will be more likely if households have access to adequate water supply, sanitation facilities, and modern fuels. And climate change resulting from unchecked emissions of greenhouse gases will exacerbate the spread of vectorborne diseases and increase the likelihood of natural disasters—disasters that, in turn, reduce income and destroy the infrastructure for education and health. If environmental sustainability is not ensured, progress toward the other Millennium Development Goals may be short lived.

PILLARS FOR RESPONSIBLE GROWTH

The goal of the development community is to promote environmental improvement as a fundamental element of development and of strategies and actions to reduce poverty. Supporting this goal are three objectives: improving people's quality of life, protecting the quality of the regional and global environmental commons, and improving the quality of growth.

The environment, quality of life, and poverty reduction are strongly related in three broad areas:

- *Enhancing livelihoods.* Poor people often depend heavily on the productivity and environmental services of ecosystems and natural resources for as much as 30 to 50 percent of their total income. Nearly a billion households rely directly on the services of natural capital stocks and intricately interdependent ecosystems for their daily livelihood. As the availability and quality of such resources decline, these livelihoods are threatened. Poverty reduction efforts need to support communities to sustainably manage land, water, and forests.
- *Protecting and reducing environmental health risks.* Environmental factors, such as unsafe water and air pollution, are major contributors to the total burden of disease and impose significant economic costs, particularly for poor people. Achieving the Millennium Development Goal on health will not be possible without attending to the underlying causes of the significant burden of disease associated with environmental health risks.

- *Reducing people's vulnerability to environmental hazards.* Millions of poor people are vulnerable to natural disasters and environmental hazards. Climate change will exacerbate this threat, with increased displacement and loss of life, disruption of agriculture, and destruction of natural, social, and physical capital. The losses are expected to be most acute in the poorest countries.

The solutions for sustainability need to go beyond individual countries. The deteriorating quality of the regional and global commons—climate change, degraded land, degraded forests, dirty water, and declining biodiversity—threatens many developing countries. They are expected to suffer most of the worst effects of climate change, even though more than 75 percent of cumulative greenhouse gas emissions have been emitted by industrial nations. A poverty-focused environmental agenda requires the following:

- Emphasizing the local aspects of global environmental challenges.
- Assessing the vulnerability and adaptation needs of developing countries.
- Transferring financial resources to meet the costs of generating global environmental benefits not matched by national benefits.
- Stimulating markets for global environmental public goods.

Of direct relevance to responsible growth is the need to improve the quality of growth. It is necessary to ensure that short-term gains do not constrain opportunities for future development. It is important to recognize the important changes in the roles of the public and private sectors. Developing countries require support on promoting better policy, regulatory, and institutional frameworks for sustainable environmental management. They also require support on harnessing the private sector to become an engine for responsible growth and sustainable development.

DEVELOPMENTS SHAPING THE ENVIRONMENTAL AGENDA

Several developments have shaped the environmental sustainability agenda in recent years. First, the September 2002 World Summit on Sustainable Development in Johannesburg marked the 10-year followup to the Rio Summit. The overall goal of the summit was to regenerate, at the highest political level, a global commitment to sustainable development. The summit was not simply an environment summit. It was a comprehensive platform for looking at long-term sustainable development and focusing on the links between sustainable growth and poverty reduction. In sectors such as energy, water, forestry, and natural resource management, the World Bank's strategies and the priority actions in the Johannesburg Plan of Action from the summit are mutually reinforcing.

Second, the Millennium Development Goals for 2015 were widely endorsed by the development community as a framework for development assistance and measurement of progress. It is now clear that environmental concerns are central to the goals, both in the specifics of Goal 7—to ensure environment sustainability—and in its links to the other goals. In four key areas—livelihoods, health, vulnerability, and participation and empowerment—environmental management can help achieve the other goals. But without attention to the environment, the benefits of achieving the other goals may be short lived.

Third, *World Development Report 2003: Sustainable Development in a Dynamic World* (World Bank 2002) provided additional proposals that support the achievement of responsible growth—for long-term (30- to 50-year) scenario analysis, for the spatial dimensions of development, and for the development, improvement, and use of sustainable development indicators to monitor environmental trends on local and global scales. The report also highlighted the critical role of institutional capacity and effectiveness in sustainable development.

These three developments highlighted areas—such as institutional development and monitoring results—for strong future action.

Measuring Environmental Progress

Data are available on key environmental outcomes that provide an indication of countries' progress toward environmental objectives, including the Millennium Development Goal related to the environment. Information on environmental outcomes, compiled from a variety of sources and published in *World Development Indicators* (World Bank 2003), covers the following:

- Land use (agricultural land, forests, protected areas).
- Access to water and sanitation.

- Water resources (available water resources, total withdrawal, agriculture withdrawal).
- Energy (energy intensity, traditional fuel use, urban air pollution).
- Transport (passenger cars, fuel prices).

But coverage and quality are mixed, as are the prospects of obtaining improved data. Although satellite technology is helping in some quantitative aspects (for example, in monitoring forest cover), information on environmental quality (such as water quality and land degradation) is hard to come by. And even monitoring of an "easy" issue such as urban air quality has worsened since the Global Environment Monitoring System for air quality (GEMS/Air) program closed.

Environmental outcome indicators suggest that progress toward environmental sustainability is limited (table 7.1). For example, despite small gains in forest cover in Eastern Europe and Central Asia and in the Middle East and North Africa during the 1990s, large losses were experienced in the rest of the developing world. As a consequence of economic and demographic growth, most developing regions are witnessing significant increases in carbon dioxide emissions—the impressive reductions in Eastern Europe and Central Asia are due largely to economic restructuring. Although the use of traditional (highly polluting) fuels is generally decreasing across regions, it is still extremely high in Sub-Saharan African, South Asian, and East Asian and Pacific households. The "adjusted net saving" measure, a useful indicator of sustainability, suggests that, according to current trends, welfare is likely to decline over time in Sub-Saharan Africa and in the Middle East and North Africa. These predictions should draw attention to the need for improved economic, environmental, and resource policies in the countries of those regions.

Enhancing the Quality of Growth

Growth can take many forms, and the quality of growth matters. Environmental goods and services have unique characteristics that differentiate them from other resources, such as the delayed, cumulative, and spatial variation of impacts; the multisectoral links that lie behind the damages to these resources; and the regional and global implications of many of the environmental problems. Those problems are usually caused by market failures, policy failures, or both. If

Table 7.1 Selected Outcome Indicators: Limited Progress toward Environmental Sustainability

	Adjusted net saving (percentage of gross national income)		Deforestation (forest cover lost, 1990–2000)		Carbon dioxide emissions (tonnes per capita)		Solid biomass use in households[e] (percentage of total energy use)	
	2000[a]	Increase, 1990–2000[b]	Area (thousands of km)[c]	As a percentage of 1990 forest cover[c]	2000[d]	Percentage increase, 1990–2000	2001	Increase, 1994–2001
Region								
East Asia and the Pacific	21.3	5.8	116	2.7	2.08	8.7	71.7	−0.9
Eastern Europe and Central Asia	—	—	−81	−0.9	6.54	−37.6	8.2	0.3
Latin America and the Caribbean	4.4	0.5	459	4.6	2.65	19.7	37.6	−4.8
Middle East and North Africa	−10.0	0.9	−2	−1.4	4.14	33.1	12.5	−1.6
South Asia	11.3	1.6	9	1.1	0.90	31.8	84.1	−1.5
Sub-Saharan Africa	−3.3	1.3	530	7.6	0.72	−21.6	88.3	0.0
Income level								
Low	4.7	0.0	731	7.5	0.86	2.6	84.9	−1.9
Lower-middle	13.1	6.0	147	−0.8	2.98	−17.3	46.0	−0.3
Upper-middle	6.9	1.9	151	5.9	6.22	9.4	23.4	1.9
High	12.8	2.5	−79	−1.0	12.36	4.7	5.7	−0.7
World	12.0	2.5	950	2.4	3.79	−6.9	37.6	0.1

— = not available.

a. A negative number indicates dis-savings.

b. Calculated as the average for 1995–2000 minus the average for 1985–90.

c. A negative number indicates that forest cover has increased.

d. *Solid biomass* is defined as any plant matter used directly as fuel or converted into fuels (such as charcoal) or electricity and heat. Included here are wood, vegetal waste (including wood waste and crops used for energy production), and animal materials or waste.

Sources: World Bank 2003, International Energy Agency data.

such failures persist, environmental goods and services will continue to be overconsumed and underprovided—imposing costs on those who depend on such goods, now and in the future.

Markets can become an essential part of an effective environmental regulatory framework. Market-based instruments that allow flexibility in achieving environmental objectives—and mechanisms that harness private initiatives in improving compliance with environmental regulations—have become important elements of environmental policy implementation around the world. The role of government is to establish a policy, regulatory, and institutional framework for sustainable resource management and environmental performance (see box 7.1).

In parallel with the changing roles of the public and private sectors, the ongoing decentralization of regulatory functions from central to local government worldwide has increased the need for local government involvement in many areas of environmental regulation. It has also enhanced the role of civil society in influencing decisionmaking.

Progress in mainstreaming the environment in sectoral projects, programs, and policies has been generally positive. There has been

---

Box 7.1   Improving Environmental Institutions in Benin

Environmental management in Benin has changed—both in process and in results on the ground. The Ministry of Environment, Housing, and Urban Development was one of the first five pilot ministries that embarked on a series of budget reforms in 1999 to increase the effect of public expenditures on growth, social development, and poverty reduction. The ministry's participation in this program provided the opportunity to improve its sectoral strategy, including medium-term expenditure frameworks and budget programs based on a National Environmental Management Program and a 5-year strategic plan for the environment.

The operational components of the International Development Association's Environmental Management Project were fully integrated into the ministry's budget program by increasing the national budget allocations to match annual disbursements from the International Development Association. The ministry's good performance in budget formulation, implementation, and monitoring and evaluation increased the efficiency of expenditures, an achievement that the Ministry of Finance rewarded with steady increases for the Environment Department—from 3 percent of the national budget before the reform program to 17 percent in 2002.

good progress in energy and private sector development. And new tools to support environmental mainstreaming have been developed and applied in pilot programs around the world. (The progress in mainstreaming the environment in energy, water, and rural development is analyzed in chapters 2, 4, and 5.)

CONSERVATION OF BIODIVERSITY

Biological diversity underpins the resilience of natural systems to change. As human pressures on nature increase, the ability of ecosystems to respond to disturbance will increasingly determine the sustainability of such key economic activities as agriculture, forestry, fisheries, and nature tourism. Chapter 1 suggests the scale of the potential increase in these pressures over the next 50 years—a world population 50 percent greater and a world economy four times the size of today's.

The erosion of global biodiversity over the past century is alarming. Major losses have occurred in virtually all types of ecosystems, many of them through straightforward loss of habitat:

- *Coastal biodiversity*. Indicators of habitat loss—disease, invasive species, and coral bleaching—all show declines in biodiversity. Sedimentation and pollution from land are smothering some coastal ecosystems, and trawling is reducing diversity in some areas. Commercial species such as Atlantic cod, five species of tuna, and haddock are threatened globally, along with several species of whales, seals, and sea turtles. Invasive species are frequently reported in enclosed seas.
- *Forest biodiversity*. Forests, which harbor about two-thirds of the known terrestrial species, have among the highest species diversity and endemism of many ecosystems, as well as the highest number of threatened species. Many forest-dwelling large mammals, half the large primates, and nearly 10 percent of all known tree species are at some risk of extinction. Significant pressures on forest species include conversion of forest habitat to other land uses, habitat fragmentation, logging, and competition from invasive species. On average, 15 million hectares of forest were lost each year in the 1990s.

- *Freshwater biodiversity.* The biodiversity of freshwater ecosystems is much more threatened than that of terrestrial ecosystems. More than 10,000 species, or 20 percent of the world's freshwater fish, have become extinct, threatened, or endangered in recent decades. Physical alteration, habitat loss and degradation, water withdrawal, overexploitation, pollution, and the introduction of nonnative species all contribute to declines in freshwater species. Amphibians, fish, and wetland-dependent birds are at high risk in many regions of the world.
- *Grassland biodiversity.* Natural grasslands across the globe suffer from conversion, overgrazing, and simplification of ecological structures.

Dealing with those threats over the next 50 years will require an array of responses by developing countries and the development community, including the following:

- Meeting global targets for protected areas, and turning "paper parks" into effective vehicles for conservation.
- Integrating conservation and development by granting the rights of local communities to certain sustainable uses of local natural resources and protected areas.
- Using global conservation financing mechanisms, such as the Global Environment Facility, more strategically to identify and implement conservation projects that also yield development benefits.
- Analyzing the economic benefits of nature conservation and using that information to design systems of payments for environmental services.
- Fostering increased investments in ecotourism activities.

GLOBAL ENVIRONMENTAL CHALLENGES AND LOCAL RESPONSIBLE GROWTH

Focusing on the poverty aspects of the environmental agenda leads to an increased emphasis on the local aspects of global environmental challenges and on reducing the impacts of the degradation of the global environmental commons on developing countries. This emphasis is reflected in the priorities of many global programs and partnerships. At the Global Environment Facility, three additional areas are emerging: reducing emissions of toxic chemicals covered by the Persistent Organic Pollutants Convention, addressing the vulnerability of poor countries to climate change, and managing land sustainably.

Climate change poses extreme risks to developing countries and to the development process itself. Climate change is expected to adversely affect socio-economic development, with effects on water resources, agriculture, forestry, fisheries, human settlements, ecological systems, and human health. The Intergovernmental Panel on Climate Change has concluded that developing countries—and especially poor people within developing countries—are the most vulnerable to climate change effects.

Developing countries are in general more vulnerable to climate variability and climate change because their economies are particularly dependent on climate-sensitive sectors, such as agricultural and forest resources, both in national production and in the number of people directly dependent on those resources for livelihoods. Developing countries also typically lack the technical, institutional, and financial infrastructure to deal with climate variability and extreme events. The tropics and the subtropics are predicted to experience the greatest changes in climate, and those regions happen to be where the majority of the world's poor live. Among the expected impacts of climate change are the following:

- *Water*. Decreased water availability and water quality in many arid and semiarid regions, and increased risk of floods and droughts in many other regions.[1]
- *Health*. Increased incidence of vectorborne (malaria and dengue) and waterborne (cholera) diseases, especially in the tropics and subtropics, as well as increases in heat stress mortality.
- *Agriculture*. Decreased agricultural productivity for almost any warming in the tropics and subtropics, and an increase in productivity in temperate and high-latitude regions, at least for a warming of a few degrees Celsius or less.
- *Biodiversity and ecological systems*. Many already vulnerable species are likely to become extinct, and some ecosystems—such as coral reefs, high-mountain and high-latitude ecosystems, and remnant native grasslands—are particularly vulnerable to climate change.

Although the effects of climate change are based on predictions, it is known that year-to-year variations in climate—for example, rainfall—can cause significant economic and social disruptions if they are not taken into account in the management of water resources and agriculture. For example, El Niño–induced variations in annual precipitation in Zimbabwe of 30 to 40 percent cause annual agricultural yields to vary by more than 50 percent, with a resultant loss in GDP in excess of 10 percent in drier years. Extreme climate events—such as storms, floods, and droughts—cause significant loss of life, damage infrastructure, and are a major drain on the economies of developing nations. For example, Hurricane Mitch in Honduras caused a significant loss of GDP, setting the development agenda back more than a decade.

Even with concerted international efforts to reduce greenhouse gas emissions, atmospheric concentrations of greenhouse gases will increase in both industrial and developing countries, the Earth's climate will change, and adaptation measures will be needed. The smaller the magnitude and the lower the rate of climate change, the easier it will be to adapt. Even though there are and will continue to be scientific uncertainties about the rate and magnitude of changes in the global climate, the knowledge base is sufficient to justify mitigation measures and to implement an adaptive management strategy to limit the adverse effects of climate change.

Aside from situations where climate change mitigation is clearly in the local economic or environmental interest, developing countries will be hard pressed to commit incremental investment resources to address what is perceived as a problem with long-term consequences, when there are other more immediate development needs. Climate change is a classic example of a stock pollutant problem, one in which the flow of new pollution matters less than the overall accumulation in the atmosphere. From an equity perspective, the current stock of greenhouse gas accumulations are largely the result of activities in industrial countries, not developing countries. Even so, as more scientific evidence mounts on the potential negative consequences of climate change, developing countries realize that they are most at risk for the effects of climate change and, thus, also have a stake in mitigating emissions. Although most developing countries believe that industrial countries must take the lead on climate change mitigation, make available new technologies, and provide compensation to developing countries to lessen the incremental cost burden, many developing countries also recognize that they need to be part of the solution to climate change.

One of the ways to reduce the magnitude of climate change and lower the increase in atmospheric concentrations of greenhouse gases is by improving the efficiency of energy use and by moving to low- and non–greenhouse gas–emitting technologies, such as hydro, wind, solar, biomass, and other sources of renewable energy. Aside from their climate change benefits, energy efficiency and renewable energy typically have other benefits: lower local air pollution impacts; modular scale, which lowers financing barriers and distribution costs; increases in the diversity of energy supply and enhancement of energy security; and reduced energy import bills and balance-of-payments difficulties.

ENVIRONMENTAL PRIORITIES: ONE SIZE DOES NOT FIT ALL

In the establishment of priorities for action to achieve environmental sustainability, one size does not fit all. The environmental quality standards of the Organisation for Economic Co-operation and Development are not appropriate for many developing countries. In fact, the nature of environmental problems varies considerably by income level.

In middle-income countries, many environmental problems, such as urban pollution, toxic emissions, and agricultural runoff, are the byproducts of growth. In low-income countries, the issues are closely tied to livelihoods (particularly soil quality and water availability) and to health outcomes (diarrheal disease and acute respiratory infections from dirty cooking fuels).

Because environmental issues are location specific, different clusters of developing countries have different priorities:

- In countries that are rich in resources (such as Indonesia), *governance issues* involving commercial resources
- In rapidly urbanizing countries and countries in transition (such as Thailand and Poland), *pollution management*

- In agriculture-dependent countries (such as Ethiopia), *natural resource management*
- In arid countries (such as Mali), *land and water management* and *adaptation to climate change*
- In biologically diverse countries (such as Madagascar), *biodiversity conservation* and *tapping of global financing* to help cover the opportunity costs of conservation
- In small island states and low-lying coastal nations (such as the Maldives or Bangladesh), *adaptation to climate change*

The following elements that broadly define the environmental policy reform agenda in developing countries should, therefore, be adapted to income levels and particular country circumstances:

- Strengthening policy and institutional frameworks for environmental management
- Getting the prices right for energy, water, and agricultural inputs
- Facilitating access to basic services, such as improved water supply, sanitation, and clean energy sources

The case for greater efforts by industrial countries in supporting and financing global public environmental goods is a strong one. Rich nations bear a particular responsibility for the environmental commons. Conservation, particularly the protection of biodiversity, is another important responsibility. That responsibility is partly a question of ability to pay. But it is also a question of willingness to pay. Many citizens of industrial countries are highly motivated to conserve nature where it is most at risk in developing countries. Tapping that willingness to finance conservation in poor nations will be essential to preserving resources at risk.

Priorities for action in rich countries include:

- Increasing aid for environmental sustainability to help developing countries establish adequate frameworks for environmental management. That effort includes financing biodiversity conservation through mechanisms such as the Global Environmental Facility and taking action to improve natural resource management and reduce the burden of environment-related diseases in developing countries.
- Controlling greenhouse gas emissions in industrial countries.

- Buying offsets or reductions in greenhouse gas emissions from developing countries.
- Assisting developing countries in adapting to climate change and increased climatic variability.

NOTE

1. In some areas where the rate of glacial melting is increasing under climate change, there will be a temporary increase in river flow and the risk of major floods if glacial lakes collapse.

REFERENCES

World Bank. 2001. *Making Sustainable Commitments: An Environmental Strategy for the World Bank*. Washington, D.C.

_____. 2002. *World Development Report 2003: Sustainable Development in a Dynamic World*. Washington, D.C.

_____. 2003. *World Development Indicators 2003*. Washington, D.C.

CHAPTER 8

FORESTS: BALANCING CONSERVATION AND DEVELOPMENT

The stakes for survival of the world's forests are dauntingly high. Millions of people depend on forest resources for their survival. Forest resources directly contribute to the livelihoods of some 90 percent of the 1.2 billion people living in extreme poverty. They indirectly support the natural environment that nourishes agriculture and the food supplies of nearly half the population of the developing world, and they constitute a major source of national wealth. In addition, forest resources provide immensely important environmental services, such as maintaining soil stability, protecting water flow and quality, regulating global climate through carbon sequestration, and supporting the bulk of terrestrial biodiversity.

Yet, for the most part, forests continue to be poorly managed and indiscriminately felled at unsustainable rates. A major problem is that forests are consistently undervalued in both economic and social terms, with much of the environmental value of forest ecosystems falling outside formal markets. Those failings mean that the value of forests is not fully realized in the countries where they are situated, and, as a result, that value has little or no bearing on the land-use decisions that drive forest change.

The forest sector presents both unique opportunities and unique challenges. It is a key to poverty reduction, sustainable development,

This chapter builds on the World Bank's Forest Strategy (World Bank 2002) and was prepared by James Douglas and David Cassells of the Forest Team, Environment and Agriculture and Rural Development Departments.

and the maintenance of environmental services. Indeed, a good forest strategy that can make an effective contribution to poverty reduction *and* environmental conservation is central to achieving the Millennium Development Goals set by the United Nations.

Achieving a sustainable path of development is a global strategic priority for the survival of our planet. Low-income countries need to grow at per capita rates of 3.6 percent per year to meet the Millennium Development Goal of halving the proportion of people living on less than US$1 a day (from 29 percent of the world population in 1990 to 14.5 percent) by 2015. Furthermore, the benefits of this growth must be widely spread, and growth must be environmentally and socially sustainable.

The "Plan of Implementation" of the World Summit on Sustainable Development, held in Johannesburg in 2002, reiterated this vision for responsible growth and recognized the vital role for the forest sector in realizing it:

> Sustainable forest management of both natural and planted forests and for timber and non-timber products is essential to achieving sustainable development and is a critical means to eradicate poverty, significantly reduce deforestation, halt the loss of forest biodiversity and land and resource degradation, and improve food security and access to safe drinking water and affordable energy. . . . The achievement of sustainable forest management, nationally and globally, including through partnerships among interested Governments and stakeholders, including the private sector, indigenous and local communities and non-governmental organizations, is an essential goal of sustainable development. . . . (World Summit on Sustainable Development 2002, paragraph 45)

Yet engagement in the forest sector inevitably entails establishing a balance between production and conservation, distributing the benefits and responsibilities of forest use and protection among the economic and social groups involved, and addressing the longer-term issues of forest sustainability and environmental health. Not only is the task of managing these tradeoffs technically difficult; it is also politically complex. Consequently, involvement in the forest sector is often perceived as high cost and risky.

Production and conservation in forests can be mutually supportive, however, to improve the livelihoods of 500 million people, most of whom are poor and dependent on forest and tree resources—primarily through community forest management and agroforestry based on sustainable logging practices. Those activities complement the continued protection of critical forests within protected areas.

ENGAGING MULTIPLE STAKEHOLDERS

Some key findings underpin the new thinking about forests:

- *Focusing exclusively on protection misses opportunities for poverty reduction and improved management and conservation of production forests.* The combination of logging, plus the harvesting and marketing of hundreds of other forest products such as forest fruits, fuelwood, and medicinal products, constitutes an enormous economic activity. There is an inherent difficulty in protecting forests that are in high demand for a range of frequently exclusive uses by competing groups within society. Consequently, a dual approach covering both protection and productive use is needed.
- *Despite their substantial economic value, forests are one of developing countries' most mismanaged resources.* This mismanagement translates into enormous costs. For example, the estimated losses from failure to collect appropriate royalties and taxes from legal forest operations cost governments about US$5 billion annually. Illegal logging results in additional losses of at least US$10 billion to US$15 billion per year of forest resources from public lands. Addressing those problems requires grappling with the complex and politically difficult issue of how to improve forest governance.
- *The spillover of poor policies in other sectors has contributed to the rapid rates of deforestation seen in recent decades.* Pressures on forests from poorly aligned agriculture, transportation, energy, and industry sector strategies, as well as from government macroeconomic policies, are a major cause of forest loss and degradation. This situation calls for a better understanding of cross-sector impacts and for the incorporation of specific measures for forest protection into other sectoral policies.
- *Forests have significant commercial value, so the private sector will be the principal financial actor in forest production in most countries.* Altogether, the level of activity and influence of the private sector in forests

dwarfs the activity of the international community—and sometimes that of the national government. Any strategy of reform or change in the sector must deal effectively with this fact.

- *Creative mechanisms are needed to pay for the protection of forest environmental services of both local and global importance.* It is highly unlikely that governments will be able to significantly scale down log extraction, unless the costs in terms of forgone revenue can be offset in some way. Moreover, very few countries would be prepared to borrow funds to finance forest protection as a substitute for forest production. To be fostered, therefore, are new markets and payment systems for environmental services from forest ecosystems and new ways of interesting developing countries in activities that will improve forest management and conservation.

An inclusive approach to decisionmaking is essential for resolving governance issues and for balancing environmental, social, and economic objectives. This approach will require proactive engagement with all relevant stakeholders, especially poorer and disadvantaged forest-dependent communities. It also will require strategic partnerships with a wide range of private and public sector actors, as well as with national and international developmental agencies.

BALANCING PRESERVATION AND DEVELOPMENT

Balancing the preservation and the development of forests rests on three equally important and interdependent pillars:

- Harnessing the potential of forests to reduce poverty.
- Integrating forests into sustainable economic development.
- Protecting vital local and global environmental services and values.

The First Pillar: Harnessing the Potential of Forests to Reduce Poverty

In many countries, forest outcomes are crucial for poverty reduction (box 8.1). Forest outcomes are also crucial in countries that have large forest endowments and countries that have limited forests. If forest issues are not fully incorporated into broad national government and assistance strategies, then the overarching goals of poverty reduction will not be met.

Box 8.1   Forests and the Fight against Poverty

About 60 million people (mainly indigenous and tribal groups) are almost wholly dependent on forests, and some 350 million people who live within or adjacent to dense forests depend on them to a high degree for subsistence and income. In developing countries, about 1.2 billion people rely on open woodlands or agroforestry farming systems that help sustain agricultural productivity and generate income. Some 1 billion people worldwide depend on drugs derived from forest plants for their medicinal needs.

The risks attendant to addressing the poverty issues related to forests, however, must not be ignored. Experience has shown that remedial strategies can themselves generate internal conflicts. For instance, developing markets for forest products can lead to increased competition between more affluent and poorer members of a community or between different communities, sometimes resulting in restricted access by the poorest of the poor to essential forest products. Similarly, a market-based system can disrupt communal systems of management by groups that have traditionally relied on common-property forest resources for meeting essential fuelwood, grazing, and other needs.

Accordingly, countries should focus on creating economic opportunity, empowerment, and security for rural people, especially poor and indigenous groups. The rural poor will need sufficient access to—and will need to be able to manage—forest resources for their own benefit. Governments will have to build capacity to support and regulate community use of forests, open woodlands, plantations, and on-farm woodlots. These should be the primary objectives:

- To strengthen policy, institutional, and legal frameworks to ensure the rights of people and communities living in and near forest areas.
- To ensure that women, the poor, and other marginalized groups are able to take a more active role in formulating and implementing forest policies and programs.
- To scale up collaborative and community forest management so that local people can manage their own resources, freely market forest products, and benefit from security of tenure.
- To work with local groups, nongovernmental organizations, and other partners to integrate forestry, agroforestry, and small enterprise activities in rural development strategies.

The Second Pillar: Integrating Forests into Sustainable Economic Development

Forests continue to be seriously undervalued for the social, economic and environmental benefits they provide. This undervaluation contributes to widespread mismanagement and poor governance, thus leading to billions of dollars of lost revenue. The spillover of poor policies for other sectors has also contributed to the rapid rate of deforestation seen in recent decades. The second pillar seeks to address these failings by integrating forests into sustainable economic development (box 8.2).

To achieve this integration, governments should improve policy, economic management, and governance in the forest sector, including forest concessions and other allocation policies, as well as address the potential impacts of economywide adjustment operations on forests. They should also develop ecologically, economically, and socially sound management of production forests. To encourage independent monitoring and certification of forest operations, formal market-based certification systems should have an independent third party verify compliance with nationally or internationally agreed standards for forest management. Certification is most useful in environmentally discriminating domestic and international markets; it is less relevant if the bulk of production will go to domestic markets that do not discriminate environmentally.

Box 8.2   Forests and Sustainable Economic Development

At a global level, the potential that forest resources offer for development is clear. Production of wood and manufactured forest products contributes more than US$450 billion to the world market economy. The annual value of internationally traded forest products has been running between US$150 billion and US$200 billion.

The International Labour Organization estimates that global forest-based employment (including both industrial and nonindustrial forest harvesting and industrial manufacturing of forest products) to account for approximately 47 million jobs. Forest-based employment in developing countries accounts for about 32 million jobs—that is, more than 60 percent of the total.

The Food and Agriculture Organization estimates that, out of roughly 3.8 billion hectares of global forest area, 1.2 billion hectares are available for industrial wood supply.

To support the second pillar, countries and donors should do the following:

- Analyze and coordinate policies and projects to ensure a cross-sectoral approach to planning and implementation of sustainable forest management, conservation, and development.
- Support improved governance by reforming inappropriate policies on timber concessions and subsidies, as well as by encouraging multistakeholder involvement in the development and implementation of forest policy and practice.
- Contain corruption and other illegal activities through improved forest laws, regulations, and enforcement, as well as through consumer-driven demand for forest products from legal sources.
- Address financing, fiscal, and trade issues related to the forest sector and forest products to capture a higher portion of forest revenues for sustainable social and economic development.
- Promote catalytic investments in the full range of goods and environmental services available from well-managed forests—including sustainable timber harvesting and management, but only in areas outside critical forest conservation areas and only in situations that can be independently monitored through a system of verification or certification that meets nationally agreed-upon and internationally acceptable standards.

The Third Pillar: Protecting Vital Local and Global Environmental Services and Values

Although biodiversity and key environmental services traditionally have been protected through the establishment of protected areas, the wide range of competing uses of forests by diverse groups poses constraints on how much can be achieved by pure protection activities alone. Therefore, improving forest management practices in production forests outside strictly protected areas is an essential component of any strategy to protect vital local environmental services and values, in addition to efforts aimed at bolstering the effectiveness of management within protected areas.

Recognizing this need, the more inclusive, twinned approach of protection and productive use in all forest types is the way forward. To manage forests effectively for all uses, including providing global benefits (box 8.3), countries and donors should do the following:

- Identify and conserve critical forest conservation areas in all forest types.
- Promote the wide-scale adoption of responsible forest management practices in production forests outside critical forest conservation areas.
- Develop options to build markets and financing for international public goods, such as biodiversity and carbon sequestration.
- Develop measures to mitigate and adapt to the anticipated effects of climate change and to reduce the vulnerability of the poorest people to those effects.
- Design, implement, and finance national markets for local environmental services provided by forests.
- Strengthen forest investments, policies, and institutions to ensure that any adverse indirect and cross-sectoral effects of policy and investments on high-conservation and protected areas are minimized.

Box 8.3   Forests and Global Environmental Values

Forests cover about 25 to 30 percent of the Earth's land surface; an area between 3.3 billion and 3.9 billion hectares (depending on the definitions and figures used). They are the repository of the great bulk of terrestrial biodiversity, with all the implications that carries for gene pools, pharmaceuticals, and other unique and valuable goods and services. Forests also contain large amounts of sequestered carbon, and their destruction or degradation (especially by burning) is estimated to contribute between 10 and 30 percent of all carbon gas emissions into the atmosphere, making forests a major factor in the global warming issue. In addition, forests help maintain the fertility of agricultural land, protect water sources, and reduce the risks of natural disasters such as landslides and flooding.

Mismanagement of woodlands in humid and subhumid tropical countries significantly contributes to soil losses equivalent to 10 percent of agricultural gross domestic product per year. In some countries in the Asia-Pacific region, forest destruction is responsible for 2 percent to 5 percent per decade of global biodiversity losses, with inestimable losses to ecosystem stability and human well-being.

PUTTING IT ALL TOGETHER: A HOLISTIC APPROACH TO FORESTS AND GROWTH

The new approach to forests is grounded on the basic realities confronting forests and the people who depend on forests for their livelihood. It explicitly recognizes the role that communities with high levels of dependence on forests have to play in decisionmaking on forest use and conservation as an essential ingredient in resolving problems of governance and mobilizing engagement in the sector.

The approach also recognizes that protection and productive use of forests must be pursued as complementary objectives, not conflicting ones. It accepts that forests of high commercial value should be used—in some cases intensively so—to reduce poverty and to contribute to sustainable economic growth. The objective must be to ensure that forests are used in a manner that sustains significant economic, environmental, and social benefits, rather than in ways that are destructive and wasteful of the potential of those forests.

A production forest that is harvested under this form of logging, although not pristine, will be a functioning forest. Such a forest is capable of generating income, providing sustainable livelihoods for local communities, and protecting and regenerating a substantial part of the original biodiversity of the site, while continuing to protect upland watersheds and the carbon sequestration function of forests.

The approach requires that forests of critical value be placed under strict protection and considers that they, too, can be financed and effectively managed. Under this balanced approach, production forests will in many cases serve as a buffer for those forest sites that are reserved for complete protection: it is increasingly recognized that in many situations, if this approach is not adopted, the protected forest areas will rapidly be encroached on and eventually destroyed.

Transforming currently destructive logging operations into more sustainable and environmentally responsible approaches will not be simple. The challenge includes complex matters of politics, entitlement, and rights—in some cases involving awkward and sensitive conflicts between indigenous groups and neighboring communities that in many cases may be equally or even more impoverished. Some forest sectors are characterized by corruption emanating from power-ful vested interests in the sector and by high levels of illegal logging activities. A major consequence has been the disenfranchisement of local communities from effective participation in the conservation and management of forests.

These challenges are not insurmountable. Much has already been achieved in recent years in the development of community manage-ment of forests, and much has been learned about governance, in many sectors and situations. Some major initiatives on forest law en-forcement have been under way in recent years, with growing sup-port from the international community and from governments in forested countries. Issues such as entitlement, rights, and participa-tion are now very much on the table.

Success hinges on garnering sufficient momentum to build a con-certed and coordinated effort among civil society stakeholders, non-governmental organizations, the private sector, country governments, and donors. If that effort can be realized through the collective work of the international community and other major stakeholders in the course of the next 5 to 10 years, the gains for forests and those who depend on them will be significant.

REFERENCES

World Bank. 2002. *A Revised Forest Strategy for the World Bank*. Washington, D.C.

World Summit on Sustainable Development. 2002. *Plan of Implementation of the World Summit on Sustainable Development*. Available at http://www.un.org/esa/ sustdev/documents/WSSD_POI_PD/English/POIToc.htm.

CHAPTER 9

A SOCIALLY BALANCED APPROACH TO DEVELOPMENT

D
o we want a world in 2050 in which 80 percent of global gross domestic product (GDP) still goes to only 20 percent of the world's people? Do we want a world in which our growing needs outpace protection for the air, land, and water we rely on? Or can we imagine a world in which all girls and boys, no matter where they are born, have access to food and shelter and have an opportunity to fulfill their potential and their dreams?

Those questions are at the heart of responsible growth. Although much has been achieved in the past 50 years—in reducing world poverty, in speeding economic growth, in freeing people from disease—the divide between the world's wealthy and the world's poor is still stark. In 1990, nearly one of every three people lived on less than US$1 a day. The achievable hope is to reduce that to one of every seven by 2015—and even to free the world of such poverty by 2050.

Poverty means not just a lack of income but also a lack of other fundamentals, such as being included in society and having the ability to hold institutions accountable. It means not just lacking what money can purchase but also lacking what society provides. So the rich are richer not just in income, but also in the opportunities that society provides: services, communities, employment, culture.

Today the world's poorest people are women and children, in rural communities, living on less than a US$1 a day, in villages across the

This chapter builds on the World Bank's draft Social Development Strategy (World Bank 2004) and was prepared by Steen Jorgensen, Robert Chase, and Rita Hilton of the Social Development Department and Environmentally and Socially Sustainable Development Vice Presidency.

South. In the next 50 years, the world's poorest people could be living in squalid slums within huge cities, where the threat of violence is merely one part of the social dynamic preventing growth. If current trends continue, the megacities of São Paulo and Mexico City will become the norm throughout the world, particularly in Asia. The strain on societies and cities could become extreme—and those strains will ultimately make poverty eradication impossible.

For decades, the main debates on development were restricted to economic development. This focus reflected the belief that income growth was enough to solve the complex issues of poverty, income distribution, and the gap between the North and the South. Today, development practitioners and theorists have shifted toward a new approach that includes the social dimensions of economic activity: from including all segments of society, to encouraging more transparent and accountable institutions.

For growth to be sustainable, it must address the social dynamics that hinder growth. Economies that grow but systematically exclude the poor or marginalize other groups are prey to social strains that ultimately hinder long-term growth. Yes, there are many counter-examples of economies that have low levels of social development but have grown rapidly and for some time. And there are many examples of countries that have high levels of social development but cannot seem to sustain growth. But the working hypothesis here is that social development is essential for sustainable economic development.

Without inclusive institutions or political will, countries can find themselves unable to make or follow through on hard economic choices. Extreme inequalities in societies—economic, ethnic, or both—can lead to destructive conflicts. And a lack of transparency in public decisionmaking—or in monitoring how public money is used—corrodes trust. All these social dynamics can hinder growth, thus conspiring against a sustainable future. What can change this? Social development.

WHAT IS SOCIAL DEVELOPMENT?

At the start of the twenty-first century, many people around the world benefit from the increased flows of goods, capital, and information, but too many others still confront seemingly intractable challenges, particularly in developing countries. In Africa, HIV/ AIDS infects more than 10,000 new people each day—4 million new cases a year. The human and economic costs threaten the region's social fabric and political stability. In South Asia—home to a quarter of the world's people—the number living on less than US$1 a day is about equal to the total population of Sub-Saharan Africa.

Insecurity and crime keep millions of people in poverty and corrode social and economic norms. Open conflict affects 35 of the world's poorest countries. At least 11 countries in Europe and Central Asia have endured—or are in the midst of—conflict and war, often along ethnic lines. As formal systems collapsed, informal systems became the primary way for individuals and groups to function within their economies. Barter trade between enterprises and people, the development of illegal and illicit activities, and connections using old communist party or enterprise networks to access services and goods have all grown. All those instances highlight the importance of understanding how interactions shape broader socio-economic transformations in the region.

Financial insecurity caused by ethnic inequalities and external financial shocks also remains pervasive. The links between poverty and inequality—and the high correlation among race, gender, youth, and poverty—are evident in much of the world. In some countries in Latin America and the Caribbean, the income of the wealthiest quintile of households is 30 times greater than that of the poorest quintile. The rapid expansion of poorly serviced urban peripheries in the Middle East and North Africa parallels the socio-economic decline of some urban centers. In East Asia, although the recovery from the financial crisis has been encouraging, more than 700 million people still live on less than US$2 a day. Often, rural economies fail to keep pace with urban counterparts because of underinvestment, periodic but persistent droughts, and rural outmigration—especially of youths.

Development challenges and their responses are necessarily multiple and interconnected. When development practitioners help strengthen economic policies and build infrastructure, they allow more people access to increased flows of goods and services. Support for education opens opportunities for new information and ideas. Managing natural resources more effectively allows people in developing countries both to make better use of available assets and to limit the sources of conflict. Funds for health systems can both improve people's health and help address the AIDS crisis. Each of those development efforts can improve people's lives—and does. But maximum development effectiveness requires those multisectoral interventions to be lodged in the social context: the social dimensions of development.

Attention to the social context has been proven to enhance development results. It means that development projects should take into account, within any given society, its formal and informal norms, value systems, and institutions. Within the societal context, interventions should promote principles of inclusion, cohesion, and accountability. To be comprehensive, development has to incorporate economic, environmental, human, and social dimensions. Why? Because inclusive, cohesive societies with accountable institutions are better able to sustain lasting development.

SOCIAL DYNAMICS AND SUSTAINABLE DEVELOPMENT

Increases in income are not enough to sustain poverty reduction. Sustainable change requires social change—with systematic attention to embedded social, political, and economic exclusion; to social tensions that can lead to conflict; and to support of transparent and responsive institutions. A comprehensive development vision sees social development as the necessary and inseparable counterpart to economic development. They are the two sides of the same coin. Sustainable social development can be achieved only on the basis of social inclusion, cohesion, and accountability, while relying on the market as the principal means of realizing the productive energies of poor people.

Just as economic development is positive economic change, social development is positive social change. To facilitate positive social change that enhances people's capabilities, development strategies must be informed by an understanding of power dynamics, culture, and value systems, as well as of the informal and formal norms of the societies in which they work. Social reality exists at the intersection between formal and informal rules. The focus on this intersection, sometimes called the "rules of the game," is the comparative advantage of the social development approach. This attention to what makes up capabilities distinguishes social development from approaches that focus on assets available to individuals. Furthermore, it puts more influence on informal rules that govern individual interactions within the formal system.

Context is vital in understanding social interactions and, by extension, working on social development. A prerequisite for social development and for positive social change is a deep understanding of the rules operating within a specific context. The rules of how to get things done are very different from the perspectives of a woman subsistence farmer in Kenya, a young day laborer in the urban sprawl of Jakarta, and a villager trying to rebuild a society shattered by warfare in the Balkans. Development efforts must be aware of, and respond to, the specific context.

A social development approach thus begins by focusing on the perspectives and realities of poor and marginalized individuals and groups. That means paying attention to a variety of stakeholders and to issues including gender relations, ethnicity, nationality, and religion. Development practitioners can thus work toward positive changes that are more likely to be sustained because they are rooted in people's aspirations.

Social development is, thus, positive social change, based on principles of inclusion, cohesion, and accountability. It requires an understanding of power dynamics, culture, and value systems, as well as of the informal and formal structures of societies. What works in a village in India may not work in the shantytowns of Mexico or in a refugee camp in Africa.

What is critical is that the social effect of economic policy be factored into policy decisions. More significant, economic policy changes appear to be more effective—and sustainable—to the extent that they promote appropriate institutions. This insight is based on a review of 4,000 World Bank development projects across the world over 30 years. The evaluation is clear: "Social development matters for project success, and there is a strong positive association between including social development themes and project success" (World Bank, Operations Evaluation Department 2003, p. vii). The more that social factors were included, the more successful the project was in reducing poverty and the more sustainable was the positive change (box 9.1).

Box 9.1   Success Factors in Highly Satisfactory Projects with Social Development Components

- Stakeholders, especially beneficiaries, participated in project design.
- The project made participation inclusive and brought in participants early on.
- Implementers viewed participation as a continued process.
- The project built institutional capacity at all levels.
- The project involved beneficiaries in project implementation.
- The project secured a community contribution to the project and its future maintenance.
- The project drew on community traditions.
- The project built on local nongovernmental organization capacity.
- The project made sure participation was culturally appropriate.

Source: World Bank, Operations Evaluation Department 2003, p. 36.

KEY PRINCIPLES OF SOCIAL DEVELOPMENT

Three key principles make development operations effective and sustainable—inclusion, cohesion, and accountability:

- *Inclusive societies* promote equal access to opportunities. To move toward this goal, societies must alter formal and informal rules that limit the capabilities of the disempowered and encourage the participation of diverse individuals and groups in development activities.
- *Cohesive societies* are willing and able to work together to address common needs, overcome constraints, and consider diverse interests. They resolve differences in a civil, nonconfrontational way, thereby promoting peace and security.
- *Accountable institutions* are transparent and serve the public interest in an effective, efficient, and fair way. They are responsive to people's needs. Accountability is the obligation of powerholders (those who can exercise political, economic, or other forms of power) to account for—and take responsibility for—their actions.

Inclusion

Development must strive to bring more people into participating in society and in the economy. There are many faces to exclusion—from women who are denied access to the workplace, to indigenous peoples who live outside the mainstream, to ethnic groups facing discrimination, to youths in societies where power is dominated by the elderly. Our goal must be to reduce disparities across and within countries, to bring more and more people into the economic mainstream, and to promote equitable access to the benefits of development regardless of nationality, race, or gender.

Some examples of projects that incorporate the principle of inclusion follow:

- *Ecuador: Indigenous and Afro-Ecuadorian Peoples Development Project.* Directs US$50 million to community-managed projects, focusing on the 15 ethnic groups that make up 30 percent of the country's population.
- *Rwanda: Community Reintegration and Development Project.* Is geared at fostering self-reliance at the community level, encouraging decentralized initiatives to rebuild the country after a savage civil war.
- *Bosnia and Herzegovina: Microenterprise Lending.* Supports reconstruction through microfinancing projects. Nearly half the borrowers are women, a quarter of them displaced persons or refugees.
- *India: Hyderabad Water Supply and Sanitation Project.* Protects the livelihoods of those affected by the Singur Dam.
- *Indonesia: Kecamatan Development Project.* Encourages village councils to design and implement their own development projects.

Cohesion

The need for cohesion—by encouraging dialogue, negotiation, and the resolution of conflicts in a peaceful manner—is often taken for granted. But the costs of civil war and civil conflict are felt not just in the tragedy of lost lives, displaced people, and simple destruction of resources, but also long after the fighting stops, as rebuilding proceeds and people try to restart their lives. The need to address cohesion goes beyond conflict avoidance. There are gains to be realized from the peaceable resolution of all differences: social, economic, and political.

Some good examples follow:

- *Sierra Leone: Building Peace through Education.* Supports the promising war-to-peace transition through a full reconstruction program, including educational assistance. The program includes an evaluation protocol by Curriculum Corporation (in partnership with Plan International) to measure the effect of an experimental school-based peace-building program.
- *Cambodia: Demobilization and Reintegration Project.* Assists the government in its demobilization effort, promotes adaptation to civilian life, and contributes to a reallocation of budgetary resources to the social sectors in an effort to build human, social, and economic assets.
- *Rwanda: Community Reintegration and Development Project.* Assists returnees and other vulnerable groups through community-based reintegration and development, and strengthens the capacity of local communities and the administration to implement development projects.

Accountability

The movement toward social accountability is a growing force, as citizens demand transparency and accountability from their governing institutions. Demands from the public for corporate responsibility in the 1990s encouraged the private sector to consider a new approach to business based on the "triple bottom line," a triple standard that adds the social and environmental balance to the traditional profit and loss.

The 1990s also saw the growth of social accountability, a movement designed to bring accountability into the public sector. Social accountability has moved protest "from shouting to counting," as citizens demand the right to know how their money is spent—and to have a voice in how it is allocated. From tracking budgets to improving the performance of social services, successful examples of social accountability include the following:

- *India: Right to Know campaign.* Demands social audits in Rajasthan to analyze how public money is spent.
- *Brazil: participatory budgeting.* Encourages citizen participation in setting the Porto Alegre budget.

- *Malawi: community scorecards.* Encourage citizens to rate their public services and make them stakeholders in improving services.
- *Ireland: social partnership agreements.* Established after national consultations to set economic policy priorities and the budget by consensus.
- *Argentina: "Lupa Fiscal" budget watchdog.* Provides analyses to help the public and lawmakers understand the budget.
- *Uganda: publication of government spending.* Encourages public scrutiny of the flow of funds from central government, to local government, to local schools.

The analysis of the outcomes of projects that involve social development leads to the field-tested conclusion that any development effort that includes the principles of social development has a greater chance of success, with success defined as reducing poverty and promoting sustainable growth. Promoting social development requires understanding differences among and within societies—understanding people's different perspectives and constraints. That means taking into account local contexts, value systems, and cultures.

THE POTENTIAL OF SOCIAL DEVELOPMENT— SUSTAINING GROWTH

The lessons of development from the twentieth century show that much can be achieved toward raising incomes, closing the gap of wealth and opportunity, and moving toward the eradication of extreme poverty and disease. Yet the twentieth century is filled with examples of development stakeholders working separately at best and against each other at worst. Governments, the private sector, multilateral lending institutions, civil society, nongovernmental organizations, and citizens associations often found themselves at odds, arguing over how best to proceed.

For too long stakeholders who share the same goals have clashed over past ideological debates or divisions premised on extreme caricatures of interactions between markets and the state. Social development offers a practical arena for stakeholders to cooperate, by focusing on questions of practical action. If social development is successful, it will add new stakeholders. It will also shift the power in development work, thereby making the people who benefit the key stakeholders. Social development will give greater voice to the disenfranchised to discuss and negotiate on their terms. It will empower the powerless to demand accountability. It will transform the top-down paradigm of development work into a more lateral dynamic relationship, with those affected helping to shape the projects and the policies designed to help them fulfill their needs and their potential.

Social development provides the tools to make economic development more effective and sustainable. Given the challenges facing our world over the next 50 years and beyond, it is vital that all participants acknowledge their roles in trying to address the inequalities and pressures of growth. If the aim is to eliminate poverty, attention to the social dimensions hindering growth can yield positive results. The evidence from field research is that inclusion, cohesion, and accountability are essential components of any strategy or project aiming to address poverty.

STRATEGIC PRIORITIES FOR SOCIAL DEVELOPMENT

The international development community needs to better integrate the social and economic dimensions of development, so that its efforts will be more effective in promoting sustainable growth. Four strategic priorities can guide detailed work on what the developing countries can do differently:

- Increase the attention to social development in policy formulation.
- Mainstream social development in investment projects.
- Enhance the portfolio of investments that are focused on social development.
- Improve capacity building, advocacy, and research on social development to build a stronger platform for implementing the first three priorities.

Although there is general agreement on those priorities, each country will decide the emphasis, mode, and speed of implementation appropriate for it.

Increase the Attention to Social Development in Policy Formulation

Most social development inputs have been made at the project level, to ensure that they fit with the local institutional setting and to encourage broad stakeholder participation. As countries increasingly incorporate social analysis and participation into policymaking, they should improve the effect of projects through deeper knowledge of social context and broader stakeholder ownership. Promoting social development principles will help ensure environmentally and socially sustainable growth.

An integrated framework of country social analysis offers a good way to coordinate country- and policy-level social development inputs. Practical experience shows that it is difficult and inefficient to separate social development issues into separate analytical pieces. For example:

- *Conflict analysis* assesses the underlying causes of conflict in a country to ensure that policy reforms do not increase the likelihood of conflict. The World Bank completed the first such analysis in Nigeria and is incorporating its results into the Country Assistance Strategy. Given the high number of conflict-ridden or conflict-threatened client countries, such analysis is critical to assessing and avoiding risk from and to World Bank investments.
- *Civil society assessments* analyze the strengths and weaknesses of civil society and elements of the institutional environment that impede or promote civil society effectiveness. They propose focus areas for policy and legal reforms to make this environment more enabling and to strengthen and harness civil society capacity.

Mainstream Social Development Activities in Investment Projects

The analysis of the social aspects of projects serves several purposes. It enhances the understanding of the socio-cultural, institutional, political, and historical context in which a project is to be carried out. It identifies social opportunities, constraints, risks, and outcomes of a project. And it assists countries in achieving good outcomes through appropriate project design and implementation.

Participation promotes inclusion, accountability, and empowerment. More investment projects are using participatory approaches
to define priorities and implementation measures. Some, such as
many community-driven development operations, also rely on community groups to manage and implement projects. To ensure that the
community groups continue to function after donor support ends—
and to promote knowledge exchange and replicability—countries are
strengthening the links between community-driven development
and local government programs. For example, Ghana is testing a
broad approach to efficient participation through donor coordination
and sectoral harmonization.

Participation has been successfully mainstreamed in the prepara-
tion of projects and programs. The next step is consistent use of
participatory methods in monitoring and evaluation. Although
participation is widely accepted, some stakeholders in developing
countries are concerned that participation ends with project prepara-
tion. This concern can lead them to become frustrated and mistrust-
ful, hence negating otherwise positive effects on local ownership.
When stakeholders monitor projects in a participatory way—for
example, through beneficiary assessments (Salmen 1989)—project
managers get fast, reliable, and relevant feedback that can improve
project effects and outcomes (Owen and Van Domelen 1998).
Argentina, Malawi, and the Philippines offer good examples of using
social accountability tools for participatory monitoring through citizen report cards or community scorecards.

Enhance the Portfolio of Investments Focused on Social Development

Having understood the intrinsic value of social development, many
countries already have such a portfolio of research and investments
that focus on social development objectives, albeit small ones. Many
social development operations test different ways to promote inclusion, cohesion, and accountability in different social contexts. It is
important to pilot approaches, but it is also important to ensure that
such projects do not remain niche operations to showcase attention
on values, culture, or the informal sector. Freestanding projects offer
an opportunity to achieve legitimate social development objectives

that might otherwise be lost in other sector projects or policy lending. Because social objectives and principles often do not fall neatly within one development sector, strong cross-sectoral partnerships need to be supported.

Increasingly, this portfolio will test better integration of several social development themes. Countries need to pilot different approaches that adopt several themes, thus integrating efforts to combine social analysis, community-driven development, conflict, and participation.

Investments in social development—as a means of promoting sustainable growth and poverty reduction—generally fall into three categories:

- *Increasing social inclusion,* such as those focusing on youth, rural women's empowerment, internally displaced people, indigenous people, Afro-descendants, and Roma. Examples include the India Rural Women's Empowerment project and the Ecuador PRODEPINE (Development Project of the Indigenous and Afro-Ecuadorian Pueblos).
- *Improving cohesion in society,* through initiatives that enhance social capital, reduce crime and violence, prevent conflict, or reconstruct areas destroyed through conflict. Many community-driven development operations explicitly aim to strengthen local organizational capacity and build trust within communities. For example, many operations such as those funded by the Post-Conflict Fund and the proposed Croatia Social and Economic Recovery Project seek to build cohesion in postconflict areas. In Sri Lanka, the Northeast Irrigated Agriculture Program worked even during the active conflict years to help sustain survival strategies and promote community mobilization.
- *Fostering accountable institutions,* through initiatives such as linking technical assistance loans to adjustment lending to encourage social accountability. There is a growing portfolio of community-driven development operations that link local capacity building, decision-making, and resources with local, regional, and even national institutional strengthening. Examples include the series of Indonesia Kecamatan Development projects and the First and Second Palestinian Nongovernmental Organization Projects.

Such investments have the potential for returns well beyond each initiative. They are capacity building for the future. For example, empowered women and youths can set priorities for the future, strong social capital can create cohesion in the face of new challenges, and institutional linkages—once established—can be the foundation for increased effectiveness.

Improve Capacity Building, Advocacy, and Research on Social Development

Countries are beginning to build capacity for social development activities so that civil society is better able to work with governments and vice versa. Given the large demand and limited financial and human capacity to meet that demand, expanding such programs will require strong partnership with other donors, universities, and nongovernmental organizations. Donors should assist countries in initiatives to accomplish the following:

- Build or strengthen national or regional networks of social development specialists.[1] Such networks can become essential partners in implementing the social development strategy, for example, by conducting independent or joint country- and policy-level analytical work or by strengthening the capacity of local consultants to perform project work.
- Build coalitions to promote inclusion through dialogues, such as those in Latin America and the Caribbean.
- Work with local consultants, nongovernmental organizations, and others to increase their capacity to provide project input.
- Build capacity among marginalized groups to improve accountability, such as the Capacity-Building Program for Change, which supports of Afro-descendants in Latin America, or the United Nations' Permanent Forum for Indigenous Peoples. Such programs strengthen the dialogue between donors and a set of marginal groups and make those groups more visible in their national societies.
- Include social development in country capacity assessments to ensure that such assessments cover civil society capacity to partner with and make governments more accountable.

The development community should increase its research and dissemination of findings on social development. Going forward, it will be important to ensure that more of this research directly addresses the needs of individual countries. Key areas for further research are likely to include measures to do the following:

- Explore the core hypothesis of the social development strategy: that inclusive, cohesive, and accountable institutions are essential for sustainable development. There is clear evidence that context, process, and institutions matter. More work is needed to show what aspects and types of institutions, processes, and contexts matter most for both the instrumental and the intrinsic value of social development, as well as to describe the various relationships between inputs and outputs.
- Improve the outcome indicators of social development to support project- and policy-level evaluation. Early efforts have identified a set of possible indicators. Further research related to topics such as measuring empowerment and other nonincome aspects of well-being is needed to ensure that these measurements are indeed leading indicators for outcomes and to clarify how they interact.
- Better evaluate the effect of social development investments—that is, how to invest in social capital and how to sustain participation.
- Improve learning across and coordination among research activities on such specific topics as social mobility, migration, and identity.

CONCLUSIONS

To sum up, social development promotes positive social change by supporting norms, values, and formal and informal rules that together result in social structures that are inclusive, cohesive, and accountable. The social dimensions of development govern dynamics between people, within a community, market, or political space. Because those dynamics mediate people's capabilities to use their assets, the social dimensions of development must be understood to cut across all aspects of development practice. Obviously, application of a social development perspective can improve efforts to empower local communities. Equally significant from the perspective of achieving results, however, is that efforts to facilitate more inclusive, cohesive, and accountable institutions can also improve the efficacy and productivity of new infrastructure investments (by ensuring access to service for the poorest) or of macroeconomic policies (by minimizing or mitigating negative impacts on social cohesion). Because social development is instrumental in nearly all efforts to reduce poverty and to achieve the Millennium Development Goals, it must be brought to bear across all development interventions.

NOTE

1. In some cases, these networks may build on informal groupings of World Bank Institute alumni.

REFERENCES

Owen, Daniel, and Julie Van Domelen. 1998. "Getting an Earful: A Review of Beneficiary Assessments of Social Funds." World Bank Social Protection Discussion Paper 9816. Washington, D.C.

Salmen, Lawrence F. 1989. *Beneficiary Assessment: Improving the Design and Implementation of Development Projects.* Washington D.C.: World Bank.

World Bank, Operations Evaluation Department. 2003. "OED Review." Washington, D.C.

World Bank. 2004. "Social Development in World Bank Operations: Results and Way Forward." Discussion draft. Washington, D.C.

WORLD BANK SECTOR STRATEGIES

A general framework supporting responsible growth emerges through a series of sector strategy papers prepared over the past several years. Six of the 14 sector strategy papers prepared since 1996 address issues critical to sustainability and responsible growth: energy, rural, forest, environment, social, and water issues. They move sustainability issues from the periphery of development discourse into the mainstream of World Bank work.

Outlining directions for their respective sectors and thematic areas, the sector strategy papers reach similar conclusions about the need to systematically integrate social and environmental concerns into initiatives designed to promote economic growth. The challenge is how to integrate the multiple dimensions of development—economic, social, and environmental—into programs of assistance for poor and middle-income countries.

At one level, sector strategy papers set directions for the World Bank's engagement in knowledge enhancement and investment in particular sectors or thematic areas, and they identify viable strategies for engaging with developing countries in meeting priority development objectives. Equally important, the papers are vehicles for drawing together diverse stakeholders in dialogue on critical development issues and aiming to build long-term consensus over strategic priorities and directions. The papers also contribute to catalyzing partnerships and harmonizing approaches within the donor community, to assist developing countries in achieving better development outcomes.

In some cases, sector strategy papers can also serve more targeted purposes of framing World Bank policy changes (such as the Revised

Forest Strategy). Although each of these papers was developed with a fairly narrow sectoral objective, together they formulate a clear direction for the World Bank in addressing sectoral and thematic issues of reducing poverty through sustainable development.

WORLD BANK SECTOR STRATEGY PAPERS SINCE 1997

"Social Development in World Bank Operations" (in draft)	Promoting the principles of accountability, inclusion, and cohesion in development work
"Water Resources Sector Strategy" (2004)	Balancing development and management of water resources
"Reaching the Rural Poor" (2003)	Reducing poverty by ensuring that rural populations have sustainable and economically viable on- and off-farm livelihoods
"A Revised Forest Strategy for the World Bank" (2002)	Promoting sustainable forest management—a new approach balancing conservation and development
"Making Sustainable Commitments: An Environment Strategy for the World Bank" (2001)	Promoting policies that manage environmental assets sustainably while reducing poverty and increasing equity
"Private Sector Development Strategy" (2001)	Extending the reach of markets and improving access to basic services
"Information and Communications Technologies" (2001)	Improving access to information and communications technologies and promoting their use to stimulate economic growth, increase equality, and reduce poverty
"Integrating Gender into the World Bank's Work" (2001)	Identifying and removing gender-related barriers to poverty reduction and sustainable development
"Social Protection Sector Strategy: From Safety Net to Springboard" (2001)	Promoting understanding and application of the social risk management approach
"Fuel for Thought" (2000)	Promoting adoption of sustainable energy policies, mitigating impacts on the environment and the poor
"Reforming Public Institutions and Strengthening Governance" (2000)	Promoting improvements in institutions of governance
"Cities in Transition" (2000)	Improving management of urbanization in order to redress increasing (peri-urban) poverty and inequality
"Education Sector Strategy" (1999)	Meeting international goals for education—with even emphasis on access, equity, and quality
"Sector Strategy: Health, Nutrition, and Population" (1997)	Pursuing reform in order to promote good health, nutrition, and population outcomes in client countries

INDEX

Boxes, figures, notes, and tables are indicated by b, f, n, and t respectively.